APPLIQUÉ
EMBROIDERY

Techniques and projects

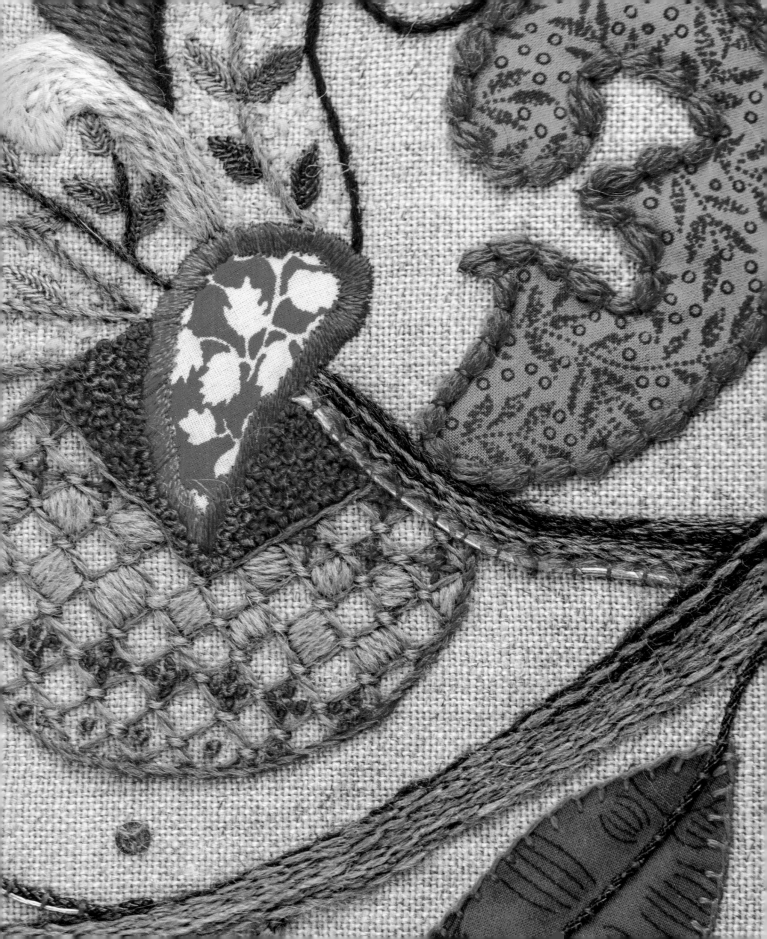

APPLIQUÉ EMBROIDERY

Techniques and projects

Florence Daisy Collingwood

CROWOOD

First published in 2019 by
The Crowood Press Ltd
Ramsbury, Marlborough
Wiltshire SN8 2HR

www.crowood.com

British Library Cataloguing-in-Publication Data
A catalogue record for this book is available from the British Library.

ISBN 978 1 78500 539 8

Graphic design and typesetting by Peggy & Co. Design Inc.
Printed and bound India by Replika Press Pvt Ltd

 CONTENTS

ACKNOWLEDGEMENTS

With special thanks to my family: Ben, Minnie, Kitty and Rusty Collingwood, Dr Penelope Cave and Walter and Julianna Heale. Also to Sue and Donald Collingwood. Patience is often said to be essential when doing embroidery, but I think perhaps an embroiderer's family often shows the most patience, particularly when needles are found in the most obscure places!

Thank you to my good friend Patricia Herbig for all the wonderful proofreading and super stitching, and to Patricia Young for marvellous help with quotes and continuous encouragement. Joyce Spearing's support has also been invaluable. I am very grateful to the lovely people who have given work for the book, friends as well as being colleagues or students; Jenny Adin-Christie, Nettie Rowsell, Jennifer Donovan, Rosie McKellar, Mags McCosher, Yana Krizka, Luisella Strona, Yvonne Rogers, Dee Jackson and Jackie Thompson. Sincere thanks go also to my dear friends, especially Emma Sneller and Helen McTeer, and also to Jo Scott and Becky Quine for all their advice on layouts and computer-related matters! Holly Cowan, Verity Overton-Smith, Claire Allfrey, Sammi Leese and Kirsty Chadwell who have supported in numerous ways.

With big thanks to professional photographer, Chris Orange, who took the wonderful full-size images in the book. I am also grateful to Rachel Midgley, at Gawthorpe Hall in Lancashire, for showing me around; I spent an inspiring few hours researching and looking through many appliqué pieces including those by Alice Edna Smith and Kathleen Mann, from their vast collection of over 38,000 embroidery pieces from the Rachel Kay Shuttleworth collection. A sincere and heartfelt thank you also to Margaret Harper who set me off on the journey of embroidery, as a profession, introducing me to the RSN many years ago.

Finally, I acknowledge the considerable influence of the Royal School of Needlework for all the inspiring and informative teaching and training I received during my apprenticeship, within the commercial studio and beyond, as I continue to teach and learn.

The hope is that this book may inspire and inform, and perhaps set the reader off on their own adventure into appliqué embroidery.

Florence Daisy Collingwood

OPPOSITE: Rabbit applied cushion cover with machine stitch and Suffolk puffs.

INTRODUCTION

*The way to beauty is not by the broad and easy road; it is along difficult
and adventurous paths. Every piece of craft work should be an adventure.*

– ETHEL MAIRET, 1916

Appliqué is a wonderfully diverse subject that uses lots of different embroidery techniques and is also often included in quilted pieces of work. Although it is, at its most basic, simply a way of attaching or applying one fabric to another, within this there are many exciting ways to use this technique. The word originally comes from the Latin *applicare* and subsequently from the French *appliquer*, 'to apply'. The word is pronounced two different ways and it seems to be up for debate as to which is the correct pronunciation: either '*app*liqué' or 'app*liqué*' seem to be the two variations, perhaps depending whether the French or English slant is chosen.

Within the whole area of textiles, appliqué is best categorized as 'surface decoration', in contrast to a technique for example like pulled or drawn whitework embroidery, which is more of a 'surface

forming' technique, which produces a fabric rather than decorating it. The basic prerequisite of appliqué is a background fabric – this could be anything from wool, linen, cotton or felt to fur or leather – which can then be decorated with additional materials. Appliqué therefore follows a similar process to surface embroidery, i.e. working with appropriate materials on a background fabric. For both processes the type of stitch chosen is an important factor in the effectiveness of the motif and both appliqué and surface embroidery stitches work beautifully together, complementing one another and adding depth and texture to a design.

THE HISTORY OF APPLIQUÉ

- - - - - - - - - - - - - - - - - - -

Appliqué developed in different ways, in different countries. In England it developed with surface embroidery as a way of decorating a design further; not only would patchwork be used but it might have a motif applied to it and then extra embroidery stitches added on top to cre-

The 'B' letter is part of a children's book of the alphabet, applied very simply using buttonhole stitch, with surface stitches to decorate.

ate layers of interest and texture. But each country had different designs, colours and fabrics that they used and therefore different ways of using the basic idea of applying one fabric to another. The Egyptians are thought to have been the first to give it a go; here it was a practical technique being used on items for the home and for garments to wear. In the Middle Ages it was also used on ecclesiastical banners and clothing. In France fabric was glued to thin paper and then pressed until dry (a little like we use Bondaweb now) and then the motif was cut out, glued again and fixed to the background with simple stitches – surface stitches being intrinsic to the technique from the very beginning,

OPPOSITE: A more modern design has been worked using traditional crewel-work stitches, in stranded cottons with metalwork and applied fabrics.

This stitched heart by Yana Krizka shows folk art influence, creating bold patterns and designs, often mirrored on either side, and often using just two colours such as red and white, which the Swedish particularly enjoyed.

Attaching a mirror to fabric

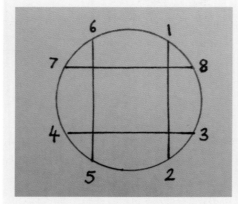

Work the first grid, so that short not long stitches are worked on the underneath.

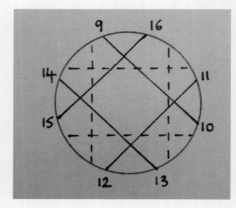

The second grid forms a star shape.

The needle comes up on the outside of the mirror, passes underneath all the threads from the centre of the star and down at the dot, next to where the thread started.

Come out at the square, through the loop and pull tight.

even with the use of lots of glue! A cord was then laid around the edge, much as we use couching on the transfer method of appliqué, and stitched invisibly in place. In Germany and Austria many wall coverings were made using appliqué techniques, a particular feature in the seventeenth and eighteenth centuries. Silk fabrics and ribbons were glued behind cut-outs from a cardboard stencil, the solid stencil parts becoming the fabric motif and a relief effect being created. Decoration – beads, metal foil and metallic threads – was added afterwards to give a richness to the work. Peasant clothing was also often covered with embroidery and appliqué; the traditional Austrian brown dirndl skirt, gold Linz cap and silk aprons were covered with decoration, and the use of appliqué on women's dresses developed from a basic craft to a sophisticated way of showing an increase in wealth and standing.

Repeat with the stitch going underneath the grid/star and pull tight, but go down into the previous chain stitch and out of the loop as before.

Once completed, repeat the process around the middle, always coming underneath as many threads of the star as needed.

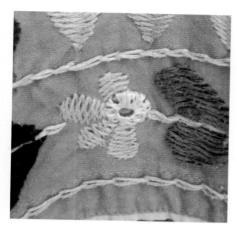

A completed Shisha mirror, from a 1970s skirt. Roughly stitched but note the combination of herringbone and chain stitch that is also used.

Indian appliqué is fairly flat so can be used in various ways, from cushion covers, bed-linen and quilts to garments.

An example of a quilt by Mags McCosher showing a traditional floral motif.

Indian appliqué often used Shisha mirrors, small irregular edged pieces of mirror that were attached to the fabric using embroidery thread. The mirrors originally contained a small piece of silver, blown by mouth and were said to keep evil spirits at bay. Now manufactured mirror glass or mica is used and fixed with a cross stitch which is sewn over in different patterns, usually with a bright, contrasting coloured thread. There are a few different methods of attaching the mirror to the fabric, but the method described here is quite commonly used.

Indian appliqué also often used cut-work and reverse appliqué techniques (*see* Chapter 7), using cottons in various bright colours and fine repetitive patterns. In Romania, mirrors were also used, combined with punched leather, which was applied onto coats and waistcoats; in Hungary the traditional sheepskin waistcoats called *kodmon* (worn by the women) and the coats called *szur* (worn by the men when courting for a wife) were decorated with appliqué. Just as birds plume their feathers to attract a partner, we used decoration

Close-up of traditional crewelwork design showing areas of appliqué combined with wool, cotton and metal threads.

bright green on white and red and yellow – the royal colours, usually with a single intricate motif cut from one piece of fabric. In North America the patchwork developed into true folk art, also using scraps of fabric for bedspreads. These quilts were often based on more geometric designs and shapes, but the appliqué technique did allow much greater freedom; contours could be more varied and separate sections could be brought out or made to recede simply by overlapping fabrics and padding. During the eighteenth and nineteenth centuries this was particularly popular and really a necessity in the eighteenth century where textiles had to be transported over long distances, making them expensive and difficult to come by. The settlers valued any scraps of fabric, which they joined together to make new large pieces, often using birds, flowers and trees as their templates and motifs, and there is therefore a strong link between patchwork/quilts and appliqué from the beginning.

Appliqué can be used to create all sorts of different images: flat pictures with patterns or three-dimensional, sculptural pictures, depending on whether the fabric is applied and stitched flat onto another fabric or if it is applied on top of padding, which can create the extra depth and height. Because of this it is sometimes used in raised and stumpwork embroidery to give backgrounds perspective, by using layered fabrics, for example. Applied fabrics can also be used within flatter embroidery pieces such as traditional crewelwork or within embroidered pictures that use simple embroidery stitches. Combining techniques within a design can be really effective and for large areas or shapes that would benefit from a colour that is different to the background, but are too big to be filled in completely with stitch, appliqué can be a great alternative. Or the

too in the form of applied design and decoration! In Siberia, the Ghiliak tribe used intricate appliqué onto the skins of salmon to make into bridal wear, the motif often being a tree of life carried by birds, as a sign of fertility.

In Hawaii, English missionaries taught the women how to make quilts from scraps of fabrics. Inspired by natural forms where they live, motifs often included pineapples, figs and other fruit but also included mythological subjects. They developed a library of motifs to reproduce in appliqué and the *leis* – garlands of bright red on a white background – are typical of the island. Large quilted bedcovers are decorated with

Appliqué based on a folk art design. Paper designs can be cut out much like a snowflake or doily, or cut like a stencil, then cut out in fabric, and then applied to a background. The use of bold colour and the contrast between the two fabrics and the couching thread is typical in these designs.

Many artists, past and present, use appliqué within their work in lots of different ways. Kathleen Mann, Alice Edna Smith and Rebecca Crompton were some of the earlier embroiderers using this technique in the early 1900s. Their designs often included faces and figures with foliage in the background, using a mixture of fabrics and surface stitches.

In the 1920s, Rebecca Crompton challenged the practice of embroidery of the time, which promoted technical precision and historical design. Crompton's work combined hand and machine stitching with different fabrics and threads, promoting a more lively and creative approach than had previously been seen.

Alice Edna Smith's work was greatly influenced by Crompton, Thompson and Mann. She believed that it was always better that the person who worked the embroidery should also make the design.

design might just need a bit more depth – this is easy to create by adding and applying other fabrics with colour or pattern, flat or padded.

One of the lovely things about appliqué is that it can be used in combination with lots of other embroidery techniques and can add a real accent or depth to a piece of work. Over the years appliqué has been used by many countries, each with their own style of embroidery and identity. And each style, be it Art Deco or Hungarian folk art, uses appliqué in its own way, using different fabrics and threads as well as different processes of adding or cutting away fabric, turning under edges or using stitch to create texture.

Drawing taken from two of Alice Edna Smith's designs.

A drawing in the style of a Thompson design.

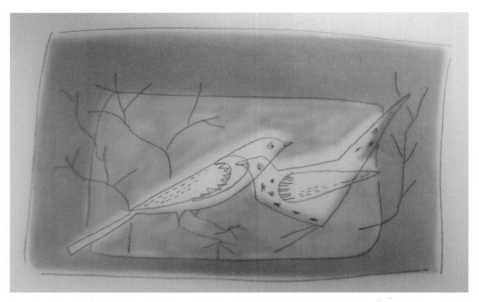

Drawing in a similar style to Constance Howards's bold pair of white birds, which she worked as a panel in 1950.

Elizabeth Grace Thompson, having trained as a painter, became one of Crompton's students and subsequently passed on many of Crompton's ideas in her own teaching. She was also part of the team that worked on the Overlord Embroidery, which used mainly appliqué methods of embroidery.

Constance Howard is particularly remembered for her bold designs of faces and animals from the 1950s and 1960s. Her work was like those of her earlier counterparts in the methods and materials that she used, but her designs were very much of the period in which she was living: shapes and squares of colour were often used.

Constance Howard was born in 1910 and from an early age always wanted to go to art school. She joined the Royal College of Art after finishing at the Northampton School of Art and was taught by Rebecca Crompton, whom she considered highly influential. She taught at various art schools and embroidery was part of her work within her art. Many of her later pieces of embroidery were more abstract than the earlier ones, showing shapes and squares of colour applied to a background fabric. Couching and surface stitches were worked in a variety of threads, and the colour of the fabric, or the weight of it next to another, was perhaps more important than what it was made from. Machine stitching was combined with hand stitches, and she had a liking for the use of just one stitch, but in a variation of threads and size. Constance believed it would be possible to work with just running stitch and variations on it for ever: 'Work it in a range of threads, positions and spacing

or in thick or thin stripes.' Endless possibilities! Howard herself went on to teach Diane Bates and Richard Box, who often use machine embroidery over applied fabrics within their work.

Born in 1911, the textile artist Beryl Dean also used appliqué techniques within her designs and was probably best known for her ecclesiastical works. Beryl Dean studied at The Royal School of Art Needlework, as it was then known, and at the Bromley School of Art before winning a scholarship to the Royal College of Art. Some years later she wrote:

Realising suddenly in about 1952 that ecclesiastical embroidery was totally uninfluenced by the tremendous change in secular embroidery that had been brought through the approach of Rebecca Crompton, I decided to concentrate entirely upon trying to bring church needlework up to date.

Machine-embroidered appliqué has been used by many textile artists over applied fabrics. This example just uses very simple, free straight stitch on top of cotton, linen and lace.

This monkey was inspired after looking at Karen Nicol's work, where bold animal designs have applied fabrics that stand proud as well as flat.

Dean was also a student of Elizabeth Grace Thompson and for the next twenty years she ran the Ecclesiastical Embroidery course as well as writing many books on the subject. The Windsor Panels for St George's Chapel at Windsor Castle and the Jubilee Cope for St Paul's Cathedral are both great examples of her work, both of which include wonderful appliqué techniques.

Many wonderful textile artists have come along since those just mentioned, including Jan Beany and Jean Littlejohn (also known as 'Double Trouble'), who were guided and influenced by Howard and Dean's teaching and work. They create beautiful, more abstract pieces of textured embroideries that are full of stitch and can provide wonderful inspiration for one's own work. Audrey Walker and Alice Kettle are artists who work large-scale figurative embroideries, also often

using machine stitching to create texture over fabrics. Walker's embroideries explore colour and light within figures and still life, and are often quiet, contemplative pieces of work. Kettle's more recent work is all machine based but as a painter first, her work is a feast of colour and tone, in the way in which it is put together. Karen Nicol is another embroidery and mixed media artist who uses stitching as a texture over applied fabrics, but also uses paper and creates more three-dimensional pieces of work. Animals are beautifully worked in bold, large designs in bright colours using an array of fabrics and materials, offering inspiration galore.

Mandy Pattullo puts together quilted collages of fabric, paper and thread. They include animal motifs, flowers and natural forms as well as more abstract pieces, some of which make up pictures; garments are also sometimes put together in this way.

Christine Kelly, maker of 'gentlework', produces ethereal, natural coloured pieces that use vintage finds and reuse pre-loved objects and materials. Primmy and Jessie Chorley also follow this theme within their work of beautifully stitched samplers that include found objects and reused fabrics with hand-embroidered stitching, often based on family memories. Many of these artists use the Kantha method of quilting, where running stitch connects layers of fabric, usually without any wadding. Designs can be minimal, using just straight lines, or patterns can be formed in the background using threads that blend or contrast, as desired.

This book aims to explore these different methods of appliqué, designs that work well within it and how these methods can be used in all sorts of different techniques and designs. Fabrics can be layered to create effective backgrounds

This work, with its muted colours and found, reused materials, was inspired by the collage-based pieces of some of the artists mentioned here.

There are some basic rules that apply to appliqué when using it within your embroidery. These will all come up within each process and chapter; from design through to application, but here is a summary:

* Designs should consist of bold shapes, which can then be detailed with stitchery.
* Paint or draw only the main lines onto the background, as the details can be painted or drawn onto the individual pieces to be applied.
* It can be helpful sometimes to label a copy of the design with colour references and numbers, with a straight grain guide on any tracing paper patterns.
* Always slacken the frame when applying fabrics, unless using a turned under edge or applying felt.
* Unless the design requires fabrics to go in different directions, it is advisable to make sure the grain of the applied pieces is the same as the grain of the background fabric. There are occasions where this may not be necessary, e.g. where fabric manipulation is used or when applying confetti-like pieces of fabric.
* Always pin the pieces (remembering to use appropriate size pins so as not to mark the fabric) and tack for larger pieces of fabric or where fabric is fine and pins may mark it.
* Always tighten the frame before adding embroidery or edging stitches.
* Start with the piece of the design furthest away, then work to the front of the design.

onto which embroidery can be added; different types of padding can be used to create height, perspective and three-dimensional effects; and fabrics of all types – subtle or bold – can be used on top of these paddings and by themselves. Lots and lots of different edging stitches can be used around the fabrics to give a heap of different effects, using a variety of threads. And it is of course a great way to use up little bits of fabric and explore using all sorts of threads and materials that might not be as appropriate in other embroidery techniques.

- There are various methods of padding to use as the design requires, including felt, carpet felt, wadding, pelmet Vilene, string and stuffing; all, some or none can be used within a piece of appliqué work to give depth and perspective.
- During application, the needle should always be brought up on the outside of the shapes and down into the applied fabric.
- Always choose a needle size that is suitable for the threads and fabrics being used. A small needle is useful for fine threads on light and heavy-weight fabrics. A thicker needle is more suitable for thicker threads and fabrics.
- Surface embroidery stitches can be useful to add to the applied shapes and motifs or backgrounds for dividing and highlighting areas.
- Stitchery, couching and cords can soften and neaten the edges of the applied pieces.
- Some decoration, hand stitching or machine embroidery can be worked on the fabric before applying it to the main design.

This example shows how a variety of different threads can be used to edge and decorate both the silk and cotton lawn, and also the background.

CHAPTER 1

DESIGN, COLOUR AND PLANNING

Colour above all is a means of liberation.

– HENRI MATISSE (1869–1954)

Before beginning any piece of embroidery it is essential to have first an idea, then a design and a plan of action or order of work! An order of work is particularly important for complex or detailed pieces of appliqué work that may include several padding areas, different materials and various edging techniques within the one piece. For simpler pieces of work, where perhaps only one method or stitch is being used, it is not so vital to have a detailed order of work; nevertheless, it can still be a really good habit to get into before commencing any project, because it really does help to highlight any issues or dilemmas, or processes that may have been overlooked.

DESIGN AND LAYOUT

Designs for appliqué can be varied and wide in their subject matter: figurative, abstract, natural forms and more industrial sources all work well and the success of a piece can depend also on which appliqué technique is chosen. For example, cutwork may work well for a background or pattern while broderie perse is great for natural images, such as flowers and leaves. Transfer appliqué works well for bold images without too much detail; simple and uncomplicated shapes work well for straightforward appliqué embroidery, fabric on top of fabric. Often but not by any means exclusively, this technique is chosen particularly for designs with bold images, simple shapes that can then be given definition by layers of padding, added stitches and by the materials and threads chosen for the piece of work.

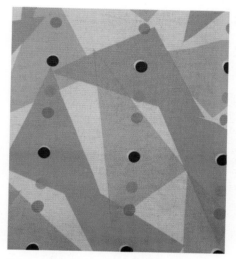

Fabric with a bold, simple pattern can be a great starting point for appliqué.

It can also be used within a shape or motif, such as this letter 'M'.

OPPOSITE: Colour wheel, worked in silks and cottons.

A simple rose motif can be most effective as a starting point for an appliqué design.

Sunflower worked in pencils.

Left: 'Pink Rose' appliqué piece, which shows different padding techniques, to give height variations within the design and also demonstrates a variety of materials and edging stitches. Based on a drawing from an industrial still life including wires, metal mesh and plugs, the choice of colour and materials shows how a design can be completely changed into something more floral and soft.

Abstract shapes can help keep designs simple.

A simple pencil sketch.

The same subject matter worked in charcoal.

Letters are another good source of inspiration.

This painting shows simple shapes and imagery that could be picked out and included within an appliqué piece of work; alternatively, the whole design could be used.

The leaf shapes have been taken from the original painting and used as a starting point for this appliqué piece.

Photo of paper template, arrangement A.

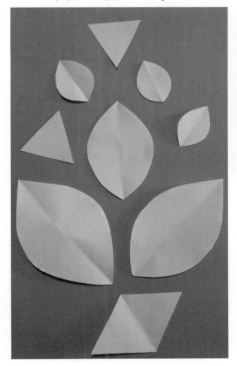

Photo of paper template, arrangement B.

Photo of paper template, arrangement C.

There are lots of ways to begin to design your piece. Paintings can be great sources of inspiration: the works of Elizabeth Blackadder, Mary Fedden, John Knapp-Fisher and Alfred Wallis are among many that are particularly suitable for this technique because of their simple shapes and clear imagery; other painters, such as Picasso, Mondrian and the Bauhaus school, provide a source of simple shapes and vivid, complementary colour choices. One's own paintings or drawings can also be a great starting point: a simple doodle or abstract pattern, a still life, a drawing of a boat, a flower, a view, a portrait – the list is pretty endless!

Pictures or motifs from a book or magazine, or a photograph, may also be useful starting points, but they need to be fairly straightforward and simple in shape, not too intricate or too busy. Smooth and simple shapes usually work best, especially while getting to grips with the basic technique.

Wallpapers or patterned prints found on cards or in colouring books can also be good starting points. Overlapping shapes can also work but need careful consideration of the order of work once stitching has begun.

Once a design gets too complicated or the images become very small and detailed, then the question arises whether appliqué is the right technique to use, rather than stumpwork and raised work for example. These techniques also apply pieces to a background fabric, but may be better for depicting fine detail and small scale, especially if a more three-dimensional effect is required.

Another fun way to begin a design is to cut paper templates out and arrange them on a different coloured paper. This method was advocated by embroiderer Kathleen Mann in the 1930s; she found it effective because it kept shapes simple.

The initials F, B and C have been designed to sit within each other and a black and white drawing is a good way to see these patterns and lines most clearly.

The rose design seen above started as a drawing where different parts of the design have been shaded to work out the balance of tone and colour.

Using a pencil can help with familiarizing oneself with the light and dark tones within areas in the design and help to inform decisions on fabrics and tonal choices.

Here, only two colours have been used, as light and dark or opposites, to play with negative and positive space in order to change the design effect.

Padding could be used underneath chosen shapes (although Mann usually applied pieces flat), and stitches could then be added as required to give further detail and to cover edges as necessary – although they could be left frayed or turned under to give a smooth, clean line.

These arrangements show how the same shapes can be arranged in various positions to give completely different designs and effects. Arrangement B is per-haps the most pleasing to the eye; A and C are more abstract designs. Arrangement A gives the background importance as well as the shapes on top.

Sometimes it can be worth working a few samples before beginning the piece, using various fabrics and edging stitches and also to try various positions of motifs to see which works best within the chosen fabrics and colours, if this hasn't already been done on paper at the planning stage.

It can be really helpful to colour in differ-ent parts of the same design to show which part might be the most effective to pad and which might work better in dark or light fabric. Tone and relief can be measured effectively in this way.

By altering the weight and balance of dark and lighter tones, a design can look completely different. Often, if a design is quite dynamic with lots of movement within the composition or image, it can

Nettie Rowsell has used a still life as the starting point to inspire her appliqué piece, keeping in mind tonal values throughout. Still life worked in charcoal and watercolour.

Still life worked in oil pastels.

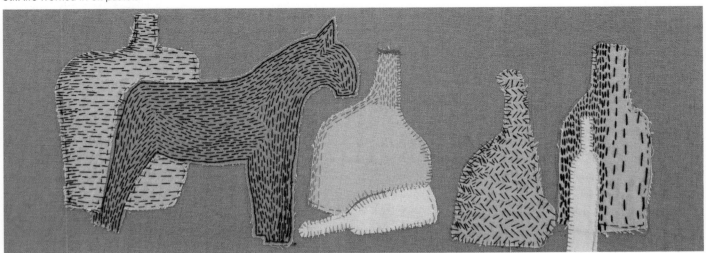

The finished piece uses running stitch over the applied fabrics, to create texture and shade, much like that in Kantha quilting.

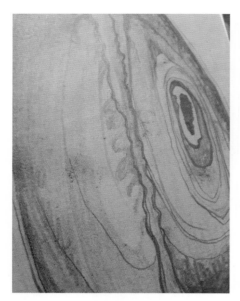

The same study in oil pastel and pen.

A small study in pencil, looking at a stone.

A sample of the study worked in applied velvet and silk floss.

be a good idea to keep the colour scheme simple. Go for tones and shades of two or three colours rather than using a large palette of lots of different colours. This is where a simple pencil-shaded drawing or paper collage can be really useful before looking at doing a coloured version.

Nature can be a great starting point for a design especially when you are not quite sure where to start – a simple shape is often best and can be most effective, giving lots of scope for decisions on fabrics, stitches, textures and added detail if desired.

This planning stage, working patterns or colours on paper and fabric, is also a good exercise as a practice to familiarize oneself with the basic principles of appliqué design – helping to decide on which padding depths and colours of fabrics and threads might work best.

It is also important to think about what the piece of work is being used for and where the piece of work is going – perhaps in strong sunlight or a dark room – and the size and weight of it. Is it going to be worn? Is it going to need to be carried or stored when not in use? These questions all have a bearing on the decisions that are made at the planning stage and can help influence and guide the design and choice of materials used.

COLOUR

There have been many excellent books devoted to colour theory and meaning. These can all be excellent sources to help guide and inform your decisions on colour choice within a design. By simply looking at the colour wheel and learning which colours are complementary, which colours share the same colour tone and which colours are hot and which are cold, you can decide on colours that work and enhance the design.

The colour wheel shows the colours of the rainbow within a circle, based on the primary colours, red, yellow and blue (used to great effect, together with black, by Piet Mondrian). Sir Isaac Newton developed the first circular drawing of these colours in 1666. All colour hues can be derived from the primary colours. The secondary colours are green, orange and purple, and are formed by mixing the primary colours (blue and yellow makes green, red and yellow makes orange, and red and blue makes purple). Tertiary colours are formed by mixing a primary colour with a secondary colour, and the hue becomes a two-worded name, such as blue-green or yellow-orange.

There are also 'analogous' colours: these are any three colours that sit next to each other on a full twelve-tone colour wheel. Using three consecutive colours will usually ensure a harmonious balance, whereas the colours that lie opposite each other on the full colour wheel (the complementary colours) create maximum impact and contrast but do not jar or clash with one another.

Simple leaf drawings are a good starting point for a design.

Stitch ideas can also be added.

A colour wheel is a really useful tool to keep by you when designing and planning out a piece of work.

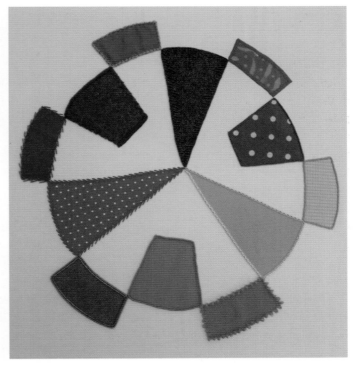

This stitched colour wheel shows clearly the primary, secondary and tertiary colours.

Analogous colours work well together tonally.

Complementary colours are opposites but also work well with one another.

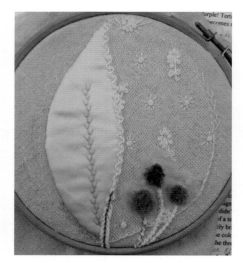

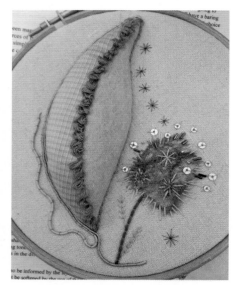

The same design is worked in different colours and materials.

These colours from the colour wheel are arranged in number order. Going clockwise, the purple is numbered 112, then colours 121, 123, 188, 206 follow and so on. Using threads in number order should give a pleasing, smooth and balanced shaded design.

Changing or swapping round the main colour(s) within a piece of work can also have a significant effect on the impact of a design, as can altering the amount or percentage of one colour within others.

When white is added to a colour it becomes a tint; when black is added to a colour it becomes a shade. The feel and dramatic effect of a piece of work can be changed simply by making a colour more grey (with black) or more pastel (with white).

The embroiderer Constance Howard, once said, talking about tone of colours:

Everyone should learn to mix tints or shades of grey with pure colour. Coloured papers torn from magazines offer a super range in varying tones. Really look at the colours and ask yourself if this colour is more grey than another. Colours in the distance are greyed down and colours in the foreground are always brighter.

Colour choice will also be informed by the style of your design. A 1930s inspired design with bold shapes and sharp edges might be softened by the use of the typical colours used during that period: soft peach and pale greens perhaps. A 1960s Pop Art inspired design would need bright, contrasting colours but those that shared the same tone or hue so that they didn't jar next to one another.

Mola appliqué (a form of reverse appliqué work) is a good example of a technique valued for the harmony of form and well-balanced colours, which were often extremely bright! The lovely thing about appliqué is that fabrics can be patterned as well as plain and the coloured fabrics chosen for the applied motifs can be softened or lifted by the colours used within the threads for all the various edging stitches used.

This leaf design uses strong complementary colours of purples and oranges, which are brought together within the patterned fabric and in the contrasting and matching threads used on the various leaves.

Thread colours chosen for a colour wheel vary considerably, but those next to one another work well together.

Sometimes it can be useful to use the stranded cottons and make up a colour swatch (as one would do for canvas shading technique) stitching colours next to each other in shade order, to see which work together and which families of colour and tone match.

Colour is a very personal thing, of course, and often the colours that one is drawn to for an embroidery are the same sort of colours that are picked for the house and home, and the clothes one wears. It is a great way of identifying someone and seeing part of their personality. Sometimes a design needs that personality within it and at other times it is not necessary. But colour is certainly an important part of the design, for feel, balance and aesthetic.

These drawings show the same design in different colourways.

On these two variations, one rose uses irregular colour throughout, while the other uses shades from dark to light in a more uniform way.

Examples of a stitch plan.

BASIC PLAN

When thinking about a new piece of work it can be helpful to have a basic plan that can be followed, whatever the design is that is being worked. It is a good idea at this stage to photocopy the final design a few times, to use when thinking about the following:

1. A stitch plan

This always changes as the project progresses but usually there are some stitches that will lend themselves to the technique. For appliqué it may be that only one or two stitches will suit the design and motifs are simply applied flat to the fabric. But you may wish to include most of the basic methods, for example padding variations and the most commonly used edging stitches. Having an idea of which stitches or methods you wish to include can help at the design stage too.

2. Colour and black-and-white drawings

These are both useful: the coloured drawings can help to identify what colours work where within the design and next to other colours, and a coloured pencil drawing can be cut into and the motifs placed onto different coloured backgrounds to decide which background works best. The black-and-white drawing is useful for identifying light and dark tones, and establishing whether these are well balanced throughout the design. Collage can also be useful to work out colours and tones in paper or fabric.

Padding plan and order of work.

3. Plan for padding

Appliqué uses many different forms of padding and a copy of the design that can be coloured in, using a key for each colour (e.g. red for flat fabric, blue for felt and green for carpet felt) can help to work out if the differing heights are balanced and work within the design. It also helps work out the order of work.

4. An order of work

Most embroiderers work the background

Edging plan.

before the foreground (with the exception of canvas work). With appliqué it is important to work out what is behind and what is on top before any stitching begins.

5. An edging plan

This is useful to ensure that the design is balanced and that appropriate fabrics fit with the chosen edging stitch. For example if a velvet is being stitched over using satin stitch and a thick perlé thread it may be difficult to put a couched edge up to this without it becoming bumpy, so the couched edge may need to be worked first. These decisions are easier to make once you know what stitches are being used where, and it is easier to change things at this stage than once stitching has begun. It may also be helpful at this stage to look at the angle and direction of any stitches and draw these onto the edging plan as a reminder once stitching starts.

ORDER OF WORK

With simple designs an order of work is not always necessary – for example, a design with only one motif that has no padding. But there are, however, some basic principles that apply to all appliqué designs. It is important to choose the right frame and then to decide if any background fabrics need applying together off the frame (e.g. two fabrics attached by a machine zigzag line) before framing up.

It is really important that fabrics are applied slack and then tightened on the frame so that both pieces tighten together and lay flat. The only time that this rule does not need to be heeded is if a fabric is being applied with a turned-under edge. In this case, it is important to apply the fabric to a tight frame so that slip stitches/appliqué stitches do not show. If the slip stitches are stitched to a slack frame then once it is tightened the tension that is caused by pulling the fabrics tight will cause the slip stitches to be pulled and shown.

The frame is tightened before padding is added. And any padding usually needs to be completed before any applied fabrics are then added. This ensures that fluff from the carpet felt or Vilene does not mess up top layers of fabric. Sometimes where padding lies on top of more padding it is necessary to pad, cover with top fabric, pad, cover with top fabric etc., but usually this isn't necessary. After padding, top fabrics can be applied and the frame can remain tight.

All the paddings are basically types of felt and therefore don't stretch and move, so the frame does not need to be slackened before fabric is applied over padding. Once padding and fabrics have been applied

then edging stitches can be added, for example a couched line or a satin stitch edge, and also any other surface embroidery stitches that are required.

A basic order of work is helpful before beginning any piece of work and helps identify any problems or complications that might need a change of material or modification in technique to make the design work better. It also helps clarify what needs to be done when!

The order of work will differ according to the design and the fabrics that are being used but the basic idea of flat being worked before high follows, and of course backgrounds (including applied fabrics) are worked before embroidery and finishing details.

A basic order of work

1. Frame up base fabric.
2. Draw or prick and pounce on any of the design lines necessary.
3. Apply any flat fabrics to slack frame; backgrounds would probably be stitched or added now.
4. Tighten frame.
5. Apply padding (felt padding is normally done before carpet felt, as it tends to be flatter).
6. Apply fabrics over padding using small stab stitches.
7. Any turned-under edges can be applied.
8. Edgings can be added, e.g. couched lines, cord, satin stitch.
9. Any further surface stitching, especially any stitches that might be rubbed if done any earlier, such as satin or long and short stitch, or anything that might catch or that is three-dimensional, e.g. French knots or wired shapes.

TRANSFERRING THE DESIGN TO MATERIAL

At the outset the design often needs to be transferred onto the background fabric. There are lots of ways that a design can be transferred to the fabric. In appliqué embroidery, unlike crewelwork or silk shading where the whole design is transferred to the fabric ready to stitch, it is not always necessary to transfer the whole design. This is because often a background might have layers of fabric which need to be applied before the design lines and then just transferring the lines of the main image may be enough, without the need for design lines that then need covering or hiding.

Tracing paper is a very useful material for appliqué as design motifs can be traced, cut out and placed/pinned onto fabric, cut around and then arranged on the base fabric without the use of design lines. In this case very thin pins are useful – either lace pins or ento pins are probably best so that no marks remain in the applied fabric motifs.

The prick and pounce method is useful for main lines and also for marking out designing lines to be cut around for a motif or for padding pieces. The pounce sticks nicely to felt and Vilene, and doesn't usually need drawing over. It can be a good idea when drawing the design or motif shapes onto the tracing ready for pricking to keep the design in the centre of the paper, so that any excess pounce remains on the paper rather than transferring onto the fabric. Although it does brush off, a heavy line against the tracing paper may not completely vanish.

Once the design has been transferred to tracing paper using a pencil, small holes are pierced using a No. 10 embroidery needle through the tracing paper, about 2–3mm apart on small designs but more spaced out on large designs with straight lines. It is helpful to lay the tracing paper on top of a cushion or wad of fabric while making the holes along the design lines. This ensures the needle completely pierces the paper. The pounce is then rubbed through the holes in a circular motion and the tracing lifted off. The dots can be joined together to form a line using watercolour paint or pen/pencil for a definite design line or left as dots of pounce if motifs are being cut out and/or used as padding. The back of the pricking shows the holes are raised and give a punched impression, which allows the paper to hold onto the fabric better as well as leaving the smooth holes at the front for the pounce to pass over more easily.

Any excess pounce can then be brushed away using a soft baby brush and the frame gently hit. The fabric needs to be drum tight in the frame when pounce is being applied but it may need tightening once the design has been drawn on. If using paint remember to let it dry before removing any excess pounce.

Carbon paper is also sometimes used to transfer designs onto fabric but this works better on cottons and smooth fabrics than velvets or anything with a bit of texture. The thickness of line can also sometimes be difficult to control. However, if the fabric is light in colour and weight it may be that simple tracing is enough to transfer the design onto the fabric easily, quickly and efficiently.

Any of these methods can be used but some work better for thin fabrics or more detailed designs and others are more suitable for heavy fabrics and bold designs. If a design is very detailed and fine, it will probably be worked on a fine fabric and therefore tracing through the fabric over a lightbox may be sufficient and more accurate. However, if a heavy velvet or linen is used then the prick and pounce method may be more suitable; if the fabric is dark in colour then a light coloured watercolour or gouache paint to join up the dots, rather than a fine pen, may also show up more clearly. Sometimes a bold

Reducing or enlarging a design without a photocopier

Draw a simple grid over the design, making sure that each grid square is the same size. This grid can be copied (bigger or smaller as necessary) and then each individual square can be copied into the second grid and then the design can be used to transfer or trace.

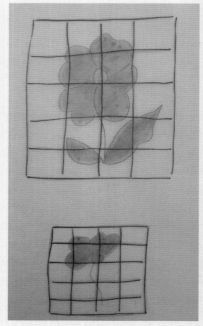

Grids can be a good way to copy a design especially if small and simple, without the use of a photocopier.

design may only require paper cut-outs of the motifs and not need drawing onto the fabric at all. This can save time and take away the need to cover any design lines. It is good practice to add design lines to your fabric only where they are absolutely necessary. Remember any permanent lines will need covering, so they need to be as fine and as few as possible. Pencils that have a coloured lead which fades away in time are a useful tool, but work needs to be done swiftly before the design line disappears! Some pens will be washable or disappear with heat, but you will need to make sure that the materials being used are suitable for this; fabrics and threads are colourfast and materials will withstand the heat of an iron or steam without trouble. Whichever method you choose to use, it must be sympathetic to the materials and the design that you are working with.

This design sheet shows initial drawings which have inspired stitched slips, in the shape of birds, worked in long and short stitch and trailing over wire. These can then be attached to the main piece of work or garment.

The prick and pounce method for transferring a design

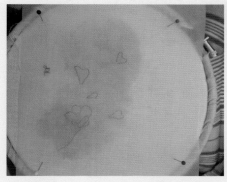

Lay pricking (tracing paper with small holes along design lines) onto the fabric and pin straight down into place.

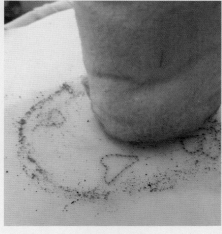

Using a soft pad or rolled up piece of wadding or domette, rub the pounce in circular motions over the pricking.

Take the pricking away carefully – lifting rather than pulling – and gently blow any excess pounce away.

The dots can then be joined together using paint or in this case a fine drawing pen.

Many outfits showing
Victoria Beckham
in the official photosh
her engagement
The £690 garment
Victoria herself
the ability to
October is
confirmed
took pla
said they
was targeted
attention on
encourage other
similar tactics.
the Market, said
minals who have
to the clues.
their bins for clues.
locals and trawled
James Raymond emailed parents.
headmaster Dr
Police's appeal
specifically for
and anyone who
suspiciously
It was a
to choose

CHAPTER 2

MATERIALS

So much fabric, so little time! Or sew much fabric, sew little time!

– AUTHOR UNKNOWN

Once a design has been chosen and finalized, then comes another fun part of the process: that of choosing fabrics, threads and stitches. Then the framing up of the fabric in preparation can begin.

A frame, scissors and needles are the basic essentials and also a thimble. It is always advisable to use a frame when working any embroidery as it keeps the work taut and firm, so that fabric and stitches can be worked with an even tension and sit well together. Scissors and needles of varying sizes are vital and a thimble will protect the tips of your fingers as well as giving more strength when pushing a needle through layers of fabric.

OPPOSITE: Grey background with paper and felt flowers and leaves.

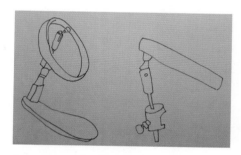

Frames come in all sorts of shapes and sizes, and are usually wooden.

FRAMES

Most commonly either a ring frame or a slate frame is used. A ring frame is particularly easy and successful for embroideries that are not too large while slate frames are square and usually much larger. Rotating rectangular frames can be used instead of a slate frame; these are much cheaper and more lightweight than a slate frame. They come in various sizes but are always rectangular, not square, and although not as sturdy or easy to tighten, they are a good alternative for the price. Always go for the best frame you can afford: they all do the job but the more expensive ones do it better and make stitching easier!

Rotating frames come in various sizes and can be bought with webbing or plastic clamps. The plastic clamps are less successful than the webbing ones, as they don't hold the fabric so tight.

The rollers are held in place by a screw and nut on each corner.

Embroidery hoops come in a variety of sizes and are useful for small work and for mounting pieces, but not so effective for working the whole design.

If the design is small, a ring frame may be all that is needed. A ring frame with a base is preferable to the hand-held embroidery hoops that are also available. The embroidery hoops can be useful for working small parts of a design or for machine embroidery but are not so suitable for the main background of the embroidery as they do not hold the fabric so tight, being a finer frame, and they also do not leave both hands free (unless you can clamp them into a base).

Ring frames come in 6", 8" and 10" size, with wider rings than the hoops, and have a long stem of wood that sits in a barrel clamp that attaches to the table, or a base that the stitcher can sit on (known sometimes as a seat-frame) – both these methods allow both hands to be free to stitch, rather than one hand holding the frame.

Wrapping the underneath ring frame is a good way of ensuring that the fabric is held tightly between the top and bottom frames. Sometimes double-sided tape can be used on the ring, in order to help the fabric sit tight as it is being wrapped, but this is not essential.

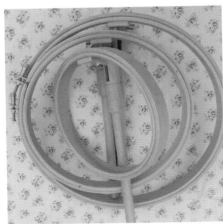

Different sizes and types of ring frame.

Slate frames can come in any size made to order, but the most common sizes are 18" and 24".

A slate frame is useful for bigger designs or designs that are more complicated. Although usually bigger, they can be used for small and often intricate pieces of work

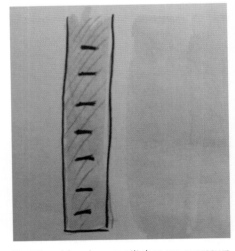

Traditional framing up: stitches are oversewn closely together along the folded edge of fabric and the webbing and should alternate in length so that the fabric is not pulled along one grain line but several when the frame is taut.

if preferred to ring frames, but they would need to be made specially for this.

There are two ways of framing up a slate frame, but the quick method using

Wrapping a ring frame

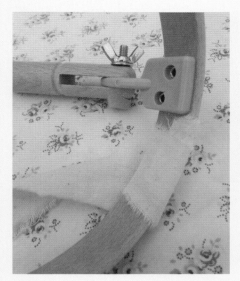

Begin by wrapping a length of calico (binding can also be used) over itself to stop it unravelling. Stitches are not usually necessary to begin.

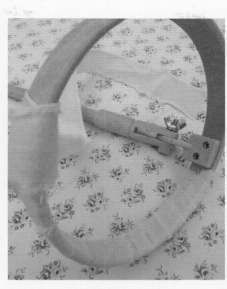

Keep tension tight while wrapping, overlapping each time.

Continue until the whole ring is wrapped.

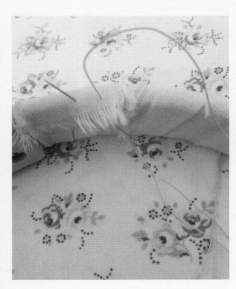

Oversew the end on the inside of the ring frame.

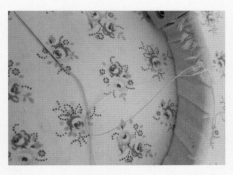

Finish the thread by going through the loop of thread and pull tight before cutting off.

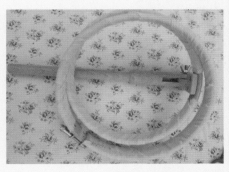

Both rings can be wrapped to ensure that the wood does not discolour the work (although sometimes this can make the frame too bulky when working a thick fabric). It is most important for at least the underneath frame to be wrapped to ensure a good, tight grip on the fabric.

Framing up: quick method

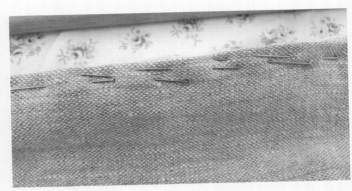

The quick method of framing up requires two sizes of pins, still using white (or other) parcel string but no extra webbing or stitching is necessary. Fabric is folded over by a centimetre or two, top and bottom.

Pin with dressmakers' pins, overlapping each one along the webbing, top and bottom.

For the sides, fold the fabric under on either side by 1cm, before placing the upholstery pins next to one another.

Do not overlap the large pins, as with the top and bottom, but place them so they just touch without much gap in between.

Any string will work, but the more it has been used the softer it will become and will work more easily, as it loses its bounce once used a few times.

Once finished the frame is taut and ready to use to add decorative and edging stitches to the design. The fabric should be tight as a drum.

dressmaker pins to attach the fabric to the webbing is usually totally adequate, as opposed to overstitching. Overstitching top and bottom sides of the fabric to the webbing using buttonhole thread (because it is strong) will hold fabric tightly to the frame. Webbing can be stitched to the left and right sides of the fabric, again using buttonhole thread and white string is then threaded through the webbing and around the frame in 2–3cm intervals using a bracing needle.

The quick method pins top and bottom sides of the fabric to the webbing using dressmaking pins which slightly overlap one another in a row and then larger upholstery pins are applied to the sides of the fabric instead of stitching on webbing. This is a quick way to frame up that is also very effective especially if the piece of work isn't going to be on the frame for long.

The idea is to hold the fabric taut in the frame like a drum, to allow even stitching. Often the decision as to whether to use a slate or a ring frame is simply to do with the size and shape of the design – a small design (such as a letter or a floral motif) will fit perfectly in a ring frame while a large or more complex design (perhaps a square picture with a border design or lots of background detail) would suit a slate frame better.

KEEPING WORK CLEAN

Once the work has been framed up into whichever frame is suitable, it is important to keep the work clean and free from unwanted marks and dirt. The easiest way to do this when using a ring frame is to simply sandwich the fabric between two pieces of acid-free tissue or old sheeting/cotton fabric and then stretch into the

Applying fabrics to a loose ring frame

It is easier to loosen fabric in a slate frame than in a ring frame (the string and pegs can just be loosened around a slate frame), so where fabric is worked in a ring frame it is probably easier to apply additional fabric(s) off the frame on a flat surface. Using pins and stab stitches if needed, apply additional fabrics and then put into a ring frame. The ring frame can now be tightened and all the fabrics should pull taut together and give a smooth, wrinkle-free effect.

frame. Once in the frame the tissue or cotton can be cut away, just leaving a margin around the edge on the front and back of the work. This keeps the frame from marking the fabric and also from leaving a dirty edge by the frame. Cotton fabric is slightly more bulky, but it doesn't rustle or tear like tissue can.

When using a slate frame, pieces of tissue or cotton can be pinned onto the edge of the background fabric or taped onto the wooden part of the frame before framing up has been completed, within the framing up process. (Tyvek can also be a good alternative, especially on big pieces of work as it doesn't sweat or tear but is slightly more lightweight than cotton fabric or old sheeting.) A piece of tissue or cotton is attached to either end of the frame and can be rolled or folded back to reveal the design. Pieces of tissue or cotton fabric can also be added to either side, again to protect and keep your work clean. This is important when often threads – or scissors or an elbow – may be placed onto the frame while working.

With both frames, an extra piece of tissue or cotton fabric is useful to put on top of the work when not working to cover the embroidery, but also to use while stitching, to cover areas already worked and to protect from any rubbing and extra dirt and fluff that may attach itself! Sometimes a shower cap can be used to cover work on a ring frame; however, the plastic nature of

Tissue paper protects the fabric from the frame edge, also keeping it clean.

the material does mean it won't allow your work to 'breathe' so well. By simply cutting a circle of fabric and stitching a piece of elastic around the edge, you can make your own shower cap alternative to sit over the ring frame, which is particularly useful if the frame is being transported around as it won't slide off and keeps everything in place. This could be padded with a layer of wadding or domette and then lined to give extra protection against the stitching. It is a good idea to put lining against the wadding to prevent any fluff attaching to the work. A pillowcase can also be useful to cover work and protect it from light or dirt.

A ring frame without tissue.

Tissue on top of the work, but it can also be put behind it, before putting back into the ring frame.

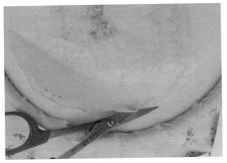

Cut away the tissue paper to reveal the design, and repeat on the reverse of the frame if necessary.

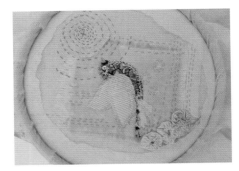

Tissue around the edge of any frame protects the work.

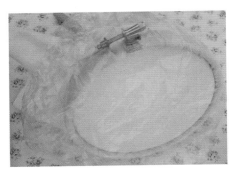

A shower cap over tissue is a quick way to keep work clean.

A wrapper can be made flat out of fabric with a piece of wadding between the two layers and then tied around a slate frame when the work is not being stitched.

TRESTLES

When using a slate frame a pair of trestles can be really essential to hold the frame evenly and securely. Otherwise, two chairs back to back with a space in between to sit at can work fine, but you just need to use two identical chairs and check the height is appropriate or use a higher or lower chair or stool to sit at!

Trestles from a table can be bigger and more cumbersome than those made specially for the purpose, but often have a useful shelf with them and tilt in the same way as traditional trestles, to allow the slate frame to be at the right angle for the stitcher. An alternative to these trestles (which do take up a bit of space) is a stand with a clamp. Wooden and metal ones are available; all work in the same way but differ in sturdiness and ease of use.

Wooden trestles can be made to order; alternatively they are also often sold with a table top that can be removed.

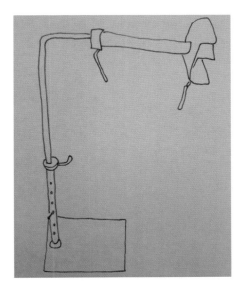

A metal Lowery stand is fairly lightweight and very compact for carrying and moving around and for storing.

The Lowery stands work really well for bigger slate frames as well as the more lightweight rotating frames; for larger slate frames, one side of the frame is clamped by the Lowery stand and the other side of the frame can be supported on the side of a table. They are also really useful when using smaller slate frames and the lighter-weight rotating frames which don't need the support of a table and can just be clamped on one side of the frame. The stand is much smaller than trestles so takes up less space and can be taken apart to transport easily.

FABRICS

BACKING FABRICS

Once a background fabric has been chosen, if it is a lightweight fabric – really anything that isn't a linen twill or heavyweight upholstery fabric – it will probably need a cotton fabric, much like a bed

A selection of useful materials for appliqué projects.

sheet, calico or something of a similar weight, underneath it as a backing before any stitching is attempted. This is because fabrics that are lightweight or of an open weave will not hold extra applied fabrics, paddings and stitches so tightly as a heavy, dense fabric. By putting a layer of fabric underneath the top fabric, it will strengthen the background, helping the tension and balance of fabrics and stitches. As a general rule, the background fabric should always be heavier and denser than the fabric that is being applied.

If a ring frame is being used then the two fabrics can simply be put in the frame together. If a slate frame is used then it is best to frame up the calico (or underneath fabric) first and then while still slack on the frame (i.e. not tightened), apply the top fabric, for example a silk dupion or linen. The best method is to pin the silk to the calico first, with pins facing outwards from the fabric and then stitching (using machine thread – single is usually fine for strength) either a herringbone or a long and short stitch around the edge of the fabric through to the calico. It can then be tightened on the frame in the usual way, once any other applied fabrics have been added as the design requires.

Alternatively the top fabric can be machine stitched (with a zigzag setting) onto the calico and then framed up in the

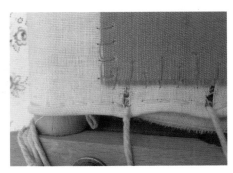

A top layer of silk has been stitched with long and short stitch to the calico beneath.

Herringbone stitch is an alternative to long and short stitch; it is slightly quicker to stitch but does the same job, holding the two fabrics together as one.

normal way, either onto a ring or slate frame as required. If a heavier fabric is being used, such as a linen twill or Dowlais then it is not necessary to have a calico or cotton backing, as this would make it too heavy and bulky; the fabric in this case can simply be framed up by itself. Heavy, dense fabrics already hold the stitches well: the double layer of fabric will just give more density of thread for the surface stitches to hold onto and also gives a firmer background to any more lightweight fabrics.

TOP FABRICS

Choice of fabrics will be partly determined by how much texture and relief is required within the design and how much padding or layered fabrics are used. There are also some fabrics that lend themselves better

A selection of fabrics, colours and textures that can be used to great effect.

Craft felt is cheap and comes in many thicknesses; it is often most effective when covered by other fabric and used within padding. It is much smoother and thinner than the handmade versions.

to certain methods within appliqué while others might be less suitable. For example, silk dupion is great for cutwork appliqué because it frays nicely but can also be good for turned-under edges, while cotton velvet is not so suitable for a turned-under edge because it is so much thicker and heavier and frays easily. Listed below are just some of the main fabrics that are fairly easy to get hold of and create interesting textures and effects.

It can be useful to stick felt down on paper to work out a design and check if the colours work and balance, partly because it doesn't fray but also because the colours will be true.

Felt

Felt is a great fabric for padding and can be layered on top of itself (much like the padding used in goldwork). It is also a useful fabric because it doesn't fray, so a raw edge can be left and is very effective when used in bold designs with simple motif shapes. It is also used to great effect in inlay appliqué where pieces or shapes are cut and laid onto calico next to each other and then stitched together. There is no turning under or disguising of raw edges so felt is ideal for this. All sorts of colours and finishes of felt are available: hand-dyed and handmade felts in subtle tones and shades can be really effective and give a different effect from the 'craft' versions, which are usually thinner and brighter.

Calico and cotton are well-behaved fabrics that can be used in a versatile way. Calico is sometimes referred to as muslin in America but is easily recognizable by the brown flecks or dots that run over it.

Calico

Calico is an incredibly useful fabric, either for backgrounds underneath the chosen fabric as a backing, or as the top layer of fabric. It takes paint nicely and is a good cheap material that behaves itself! It is available in different weights but is usually cream in colour with small brown dots. It can be bought either pre-washed, so it is softer to the touch, or with a size on it (a bit like a glue or a spray starch), which makes it a bit stiffer.

Cotton

Cotton is similar to calico but without the brown freckle-like dots that calico has. It is useful as a background if the top fabric is thin or light coloured, because there are no speckles to show through! Cotton also comes in various colours and patterns, partly because it is so popular within quilting and patchwork where it is helpful for the cotton fabrics to all be the same weight but to come in hundreds of

Quilting fabrics can be bought in small pieces, which can be ideal for appliqué.

Sheer fabrics add perspective and dimension effectively, and are essential in shadow-work appliqué.

Silk dupion comes in an array of colours and even patterns.

patterns and colours. These quilting fabrics work well for appliqué because they are a good weight and do not move and wriggle but will stay flat. They can be layered or the edges can be turned under easily because the fabric is not too thick. Edges don't fray too badly so it can be cut to size easily and edged with a couched line or stitching over the top; however, cotton fabric does take Bondaweb (and glue!) easily too. It sits over felt padding nicely and can be stuffed without stretching and changing shape.

Organdie and organza
Organzas and organdies are very useful for layered backgrounds or for areas where a translucent effect is desired. They can be put on top of another fabric, or fabric can be cut away behind the organza to leave a window. Cotton organdie is stiffer and stays in place more easily, while organza is more moveable, slightly shinier and less matt than organdie. The cotton organdie

is used for shadow-work where areas of appliqué can be attached using pin stitch.

Silk dupion
Silk dupion has a similar weight to cotton but is less matt with a slight sheen to it. It has a slight slub, which gives a texture (some dupions have more slub than others) and it comes in a wide variety of colours. Some silk dupion is woven with a different colour weft to the warp, to give a two-tone fabric which can be most effective. For example, red thread for the weft and black for the warp threads gives a two-tone fabric, which changes depending how you look at it. Silk dupion works very well within most appliqué techniques, as it is not bulky and does not stretch or move. It does fray, however, which can be dealt with by adding a fine line of watered-down glue around the edge to be cut. Equally, the frays can be very effective for a frayed edge or when used in cutwork/reverse appliqué.

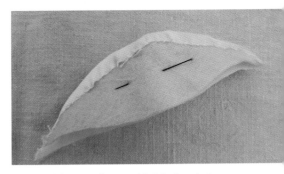
White silk is turned around felt before being attached to the background fabric, to ensure the edges do not show through to the front of the motif.

Velvet can add a lovely texture and opulence to a design.

Sateen comes in lots of colours and its shiny front can be an added bonus to a design.

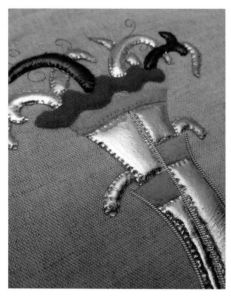

This example by Rosie McKellar shows the leather applied over felt padding and edged in places with pearl purl gold thread.

Linen is another well-behaved and versatile fabric, available in an assortment of weights and colours.

Velvet

Velvet is particularly effective when height and texture is required. Velvet can fray easily, particularly cotton velvet, which is thicker and heavier than silk or synthetic alternatives, but cotton velvet may still be easier to use as it doesn't move and stretch like the others can do. Velevet doesn't work so well as a turned-under edge because of the bulk, but is great when a cord or satin stitch is added along the edge. It is also effective within cutwork/ reverse appliqué to give texture, and can be applied over padding to give high relief.

Linen

Linen adds a lovely grain and matt finish to a design. It comes in various different weights; something with a particularly open weave like an Edinburgh linen (or duck cotton, alternative to linen) is sometimes better avoided if motifs are small, because it frays more easily – although applying Bondaweb or Mistyfuse can solve this problem. It works particularly well as a background fabric too and takes paint very well. Colours tend to be subtle and are useful for designs that include natural and floral motifs but linens can also be a good choice as a background for shiny, bright colours applied on top.

Sateen

Sateen is a useful fabric; often used for curtain interlining, it is slightly more stretchy than calico and can be very useful when a smooth, less matt surface is required. It has a diagonal grain line on the front and a weft/warp weave on the back. It is also much less expensive than cottons, silks and linens.

Leather

Kid leather is used often within goldwork and metalwork but can also be used within other techniques, such as appliqué. It can be applied flat or over padding, depending on the effect required. It comes in a huge variety of colours and can be stitched down in the same way as felt padding, using small stab stitches.

Net is often avoided as being a bit tacky or stiff but it can be fun in cutwork/reverse appliqué as an added layer or to give added dimension to a design, much like the sheer fabrics do.

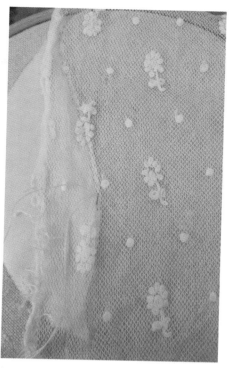

Lace is added and then cut away once it has been stitched in place.

Net

Net is a useful material for adding texture to a design or to trap threads or fabrics behind, using it as a net or mesh. Lots of colours are available and because it is quite static, it doesn't move around and misbehave!

A useful method to use when applying net, lace or even jersey fabric can be to stitch the applied net down first and then cut flush against the stitching, instead of cutting the shape out first. This method of cutting after stitching can help the net stay put and not move so much. It is usually a good idea to tack the net as well as pinning to ensure it stays put when stitching.

Bondaweb

Bondaweb can be a useful medium for appliqué. It comes in different weights and is backed with paper on one side, but both sides stick to fabric. The wrong side of the fabric is ironed to the Bondaweb and then once the shape or motif is cut out the paper backing is removed and the motif ironed onto the background fabric. It is particularly useful to stop fraying or when using multiple motifs that need to be absolutely flat. Be careful if stitching through it, as the needle may become quite sticky! An alternative to Bondaweb is Mistyfuse, which has no paper backing.

Vilene

Vilene is a bit like a cardboard and used in a similar way as Bondaweb, in order to strengthen or stiffen a fabric, but is made of fabric not paper, is not adhesive, and can be washed. It comes in different weights, but usually in white colour only.

THREADS

The list of threads that can be used within appliqué is endless. Really anything can be used – and not only something that will fit through a needle! Threads such as strings, metals and fragile or particularly heavy threads can be laid onto the design and couched over rather than used to stitch through the fabrics. This means that appliqué can become a very creative and expressive technique, using materials that might not be appropriate in many other embroidery techniques. It is important to remember why you are choosing a particular thread or fabric, however, and to use it not simply because it is unusual or interesting, but because it will enhance the design!

Stranded cotton threads

Stranded cottons are incredibly useful. They are made of six strands of thread that are put together but not twisted; this means that the strands can be easily separated and used in the needle in any number required. One strand of thread would usually be used in a No. 12 or 10 embroidery needle, while six strands would need something bigger like a No. 3 embroidery or a No. 24 chenille needle. When separating the strands, it is important that to take each strand separately, by holding one strand and pulling the other strands vertically down. If more than one strand is being used, these need to be pulled apart and then added together again so that the strands lie flat and not twisted.

A card is helpful to wind threads around, as it reduces tangles in the thread, making it easy to unwind and cut a length, but it does leave kinks in the thread nearest to the card, which can be annoying.

Using Bondaweb

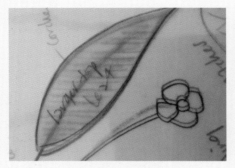

Draw around the motif or shape from the original design onto tracing paper.

Once the Bondaweb has been ironed onto the fabric (take care it is the correct way round), place the tracing paper shape onto the Bondaweb.

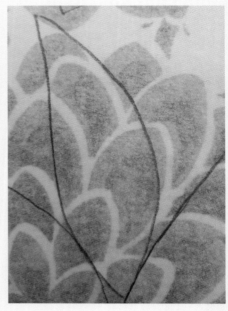

Draw around the motif.

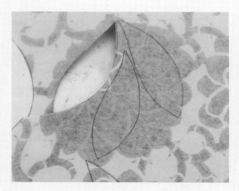

Cut out the motif from the Bondaweb fabric.

Peel off the paper backing – it is important not to do this until now, as the motif is much easier to cut out when the paper backing is still in place.

Iron into place onto the background fabric.

The completed motif is stuck to the background fabric and ready for stab stitching and other edging stitches.

Always cut lengths of thread about wrist to elbow length to avoid the thread becoming fluffy, worn or tangled – unless the thread is being couched, in which case it should be whatever length is required for the design line being worked.

Ver à soie

Ver à soie is a French thread (as the name suggests) that is very similar to stranded cotton, except that it is made of silk, not cotton. It behaves well and has a higher sheen than the cotton alternatives, which can be useful if you are using lots of silk and shiny fabrics, but also to give a contrast perhaps to a linen or wool fabric. It also comes in a variety of colours.

Superfine silk is also useful for couching threads without such a noticeable stitch. Worked over gimp, for example, it is almost invisible when the same colour thread is used. It is also great for adding wisps or very fine lines of stitching.

Wools

Appletons crewel wool is most commonly used, as it is finer than the tapestry alternative. It comes in skeins and also larger hanks. Thread length is kept as with stranded cotton, to avoid fluffing and untwisting. Appletons wool does sometimes vary in thickness, so sometimes a thread length may need to be cut to avoid a thicker or thinner part of the wool; this is because it is traditionally spun and can

add to an effect, but is something to be aware of.

Other crewel wools are available and are probably a better choice if you want a very smooth and even wool thread; however, the colour choice is more limited. Some makes of wool only come in variegated or space dyed shades while others have more block colours. The Australian Gumnuts yarn is lovely to use, but variegated. Langley Threads also manufacture a beautiful range of fine crewel wool, which is very soft and comes in block colours rather than space dyed or variegated. There are other independent ranges available, such as Strand embroidery yarn, based in New Zealand, who spin and dye a mix of mohair and wool, with a slightly thicker, more pronounced twist than the alternatives but equally lovely to use. It is important to choose the right thread for the effect you are trying to achieve. For example, if a long and short stitched edge is being worked, then a smooth wool

Stranded cottons come in a wide variety of colours and can be wound onto a card or bobbin or left in the skein.

Silk threads come in all sorts of twists, colours and makes. Some of the antique ones can be lovely but watch out for those that have rotted, as these will break easily.

Langley Superfine Silk thread comes in a wide selection of colours and is not as bouncy as some other silks.

Appletons wool comes in a vast array of colours and is a traditional wool choice.

A mixture of wools is available, depending on the effect that is required.

Darning wools tend to be finer than crewel wool.

will be more effective, but for a button-hole edge a twisted wool might be a better choice.

Perlé and coton à broder

Perlé is a twisted, shiny thread that shows each stitch, unlike the flatter stranded cottons where stitches blend into one another more easily. *Coton à broder* thread is also more twisted and therefore sits proud and more raised than the stranded cottons (and silk alternatives). Perlé and *coton à broder* cannot be split apart like stranded cotton can. Strands are 4 ply, i.e. made of four strands twisted together. They come in various thicknesses: the lower the number, the thicker the thread. For example No. 16 is heavier or thicker than a No. 25 *coton à broder*.

Perlé threads come on a reel in a variety of colours and *coton à broder* usually comes as a skein. They are often used in whitework and for needlelace within raised embroidery.

Coton floche

Floche is similar to *coton à broder* and perlé in that it cannot be separated. It is 5 ply but only comes in one thickness, a No.16 (not to be confused with the *coton à broder* No.16 which is a different weight!). *Floche* is not as tightly twisted as the *coton à broder*; it is a softer thread – more like the stranded cottons – which means it sits flatter than the *coton à broder* but still has a twist. It is used mostly in whitework techniques but can be a useful thread for something in between a high twist like a perlé and a non-twisted thread like a stranded cotton.

Chenilles and chainettes

Textured threads can be really useful for couching over, to give added texture or shine. Chenille thread can be difficult to stitch with because it is prone to breaking or wearing through the needle and fabric, to leave a skinny thread without the chenille velvet! It often comes space dyed in various colours. Chainettes come as flat or round shaped thread and are shiny; almost like a ribbon made of small chain stitches,

Chainettes and chenilles often come in mixed packs of thread, which can be useful as for appliqué projects, as often it is only small amounts or short lengths that are required.

they move around a curve beautifully and give a much shinier appearance than other threads. They tend to fray easily, so need to be plunged to the back of the work, and are best couched down for the same reason as the chenille.

Gimp

Gimp thread is a round yarn, consisting of a cotton core that is wrapped with fine rayon thread (much like gold threads, such as passing or Japanese thread, have a core of cotton that is then wrapped with gold or another coloured metal). It is not always easy to get hold of, but is a lovely addition to appliqué work due to its shine and raised, round effect – rather like a cord, but smooth rather than twisted. It is sometimes known as a viscose gimp but is also available in silk too. It is used within raised and stumpwork as well as for tassel heads, but is also great for couching around an applied motif, flat or padded. It is available in different thicknesses, but the medium weight is particularly useful for most appliqué projects and it comes in various colours, shaded or flat colour.

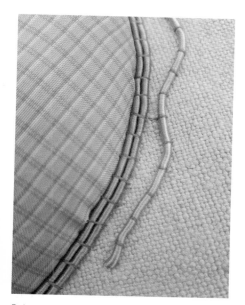

Pale green gimp is used here against a highly padded area of carpet felt. It is couched over with one strand of stranded cotton, although sometimes a fine silk or rayon thread is used to make the couching threads almost entirely invisible.

Rosie McKellar's piece shows pearl purl edging around applied leather, in differing thicknesses.

Rosie's clouds are edged in twist, stitched around a net cloud on top of felt.

A variety of metal threads that can be used within appliqué.

Gütermanns thread is a good all-round thread, which can then be covered by more decorative stitches and threads.

Machine thread

Various machine threads are available and come in cotton or polyester. Gütermanns thread also comes in different materials but the polyester is often the best for tacking and holding edges on a motif, for example for use in stab stitches or slip stitches on a turned edge. It is stronger and slightly finer than one strand of stranded cotton and comes in all colours, so it can be matched to fabric and easily covered by an edge.

Metalwork threads

A vast selection of metal threads is available and used predominantly within goldwork embroidery, but they are also used within other techniques such as creative metalwork embroidery and raised and stumpwork embroidery. They are also used as highlights or details within all sorts of other techniques.

A full description of metal threads and their uses is beyond the scope of this book, but the threads with a core of cotton, wrapped with a metal thread are particularly suitable for appliqué, for example, passings, twists and Rococo threads. These come in different thicknesses and are couched down, with a Gütermanns thread or a single strand of stranded cotton that has been waxed to take away fluff and make slightly stronger. These threads are often couched against a motif edge

before the ends are plunged to the back of the work. Pearl purl metal thread is also used to couch against edges but this does not have a core of thread running through the middle, so it can be cut rather than plunged at the ends. It also comes in various thicknesses.

Buttonhole thread

Buttonhole thread is particularly useful when using metal threads or gimp that need plunging so that the ends of the threads are taken to the back of the work. It is a strong thread that can take a lot of pull and stress on it. Buttonhole thread is also therefore useful for herringboning work to mountboard, as it can take the pull that is needed to get the work tight. The thread comes in different colours but most commonly the cream/beige is used and isn't usually used for decorative stitch

This leaf sampler shows how the metal threads are used to give edges against the motif. They can be used alone or mixed with other threads and edging techniques.

1. Couched Japanese thread; plunged at the centre vein line.
2. Couched Japanese and one row of Rococo. Middle vein line in silver super pearl purl.
3. Two rows of separately couched twist; green 3 ply and gold medium Rococo.
4. Couched stranded cotton. Middle vein line in medium Rococo.

This technique of using the buttonhole thread to take the top threads through to the back of the embroidery is called a 'lasso'.

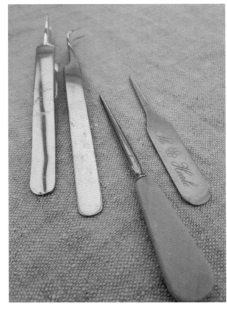

A selection of embroidery essentials, including more unusual tools like the stiletto and the mellor, and indeed a pair of tweezers.

but for more practical purposes. When used for plunging threads, both ends of the buttonhole thread are threaded through the eye of a large chenille needle and the loop of the thread is pulled over the end of the gimp or metal thread ends; then this loop pulls the metal or gimp thread through the fabric to the back of the work, ready to be tied back.

USEFUL TOOLS

NEEDLES

There are three types of main needle that are used within embroidery. These are embroidery, chenille and tapestry needles. John James needles are particularly well made and come in various packs, mixed sizes and on cards, in envelopes or in pebble-shaped boxes.

Embroidery needles have a small eye and are sharp. The smallest are No. 12 and then No. 10, which are useful for machine or silk thread, or a single strand of stranded cotton.

Chenille needles are slightly shorter and thicker than the embroidery needles. They have a larger eye although still with a sharp point and can be useful not only for thicker threads, but also for plunging couched threads to the back of the work.

Tapestry needles look very similar to chenille needles but do not have a sharp point; they are blunt and really only used for canvas and more open weave fabrics, within techniques such as canvas stitches or shading, blackwork and cross stitch. They can also be useful for pushing threads together and also for stitches that require weaving around a stitch rather than going in and out of the fabric.

Other types of needles are available, such as sharps, beading and darners, but

Embroidery needles are the finest available for embroidery (unless you are using a beading needle). The finest is a No. 12 and the largest a No. 3.

Chenille needles start at a No. 26 (smallest) and range upwards in even numbers only to a No. 18 (largest). No. 24 is commonly used for stitching, while a No. 18 or 20 is very useful for plunging.

Tapestry needles are numbered similarly to chenille, starting at a No. 28 (finest) to a No. 18 (largest).

Needles can be kept in cases or on cards and in boxes in tins, or in wooden holders.

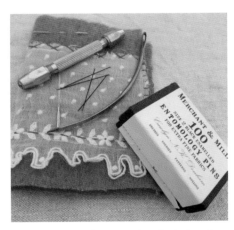

The biggest needle around, called a bracing needle, shown here with a 'pricker' (a handle into which to put a needle when pricking out a design).

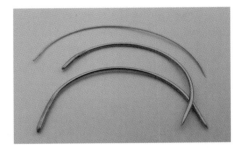

Curved needles are particularly useful when mounting and come in different sizes and lengths.

these are used less in embroidery techniques. Curved needles are very useful when mounting a piece of work over a board and for some other making up techniques, but are not usually required for the embroidery itself.

A bracing needle is a huge needle that is particularly useful for framing up when using webbing, in order to stitch the string through the webbing or fabric.

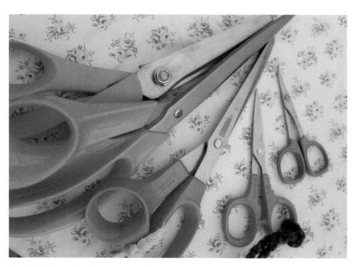

A selection of scissors – useful for any embroidery kit.

A selection of pins.

OTHER ESSENTIALS

Scissors

There are many scissors available; some jobs require large scissors while others need tiny, sharp blades. It is a good idea to have a large pair for fabric, a pair for paper and a small pair for embroidery thread. It can also be useful to have a medium-sized pair for cutting smaller, more intricate shapes and perhaps also a small pair for cutting wire and metal threads, so as not to blunt your embroidery pair! Like many things, scissors come in all sorts of ranges and price brackets but a thin blade is essential for embroidery.

The Janome embroidery scissors – with either a curved or straight blade – are excellent, because of their thin metal blade that is not too chunky. As long as the blade is thin it will allow the scissors to get as close as possible to the thread, which will make any job much easier and result in more accurate cutting.

Mellor

A mellor is a laying tool, made from metal, which helps push threads together or keep them from getting tangled without having to touch and prod the thread with your fingers! Predominantly used in goldwork it is also useful for other techniques. It has a flat, rounded end for pushing against threads, especially couched threads that need to sit close to one another, and a pointed end, which can be used to make a hole in the fabric through which to plunge threads.

Stiletto

A stiletto also has a sharp, pointed end, for making holes and eyelets in the fabric, but can be useful for plunging threads as well. It is predominantly a whitework tool for creating eyelets but is useful for appliqué techniques as well.

Tweezers

Tweezers are useful for squeezing threads together and for pushing into place as well as holding to get a more precise placement. They come curved or straight, with fine metal ends that allow for precision.

Pins

Pins come in many lengths and sizes. Glass-headed pins (with a coloured bead at the top) are useful for mounting and most projects. Dressmakers' pins with a small head and no colour are particularly useful when using the quick method of framing up, and lace and ento (entomology) pins are particularly handy when pinning fine fabrics, as they don't leave a mark.

A selection of thimbles and adhesive leather dots.

The prick and pounce method is the traditional way of transferring a design onto fabric.

Thimble

A thimble is pretty essential for all stitching jobs, but particularly when working through padding or slightly stiffer and heavier fabrics and materials. It is also helpful to prevent you fingertips from getting sore.

As well as metal thimbles, leather and plastic ones are available. Also useful are small adhesive leather dots, which can be stuck onto the pad of a finger; these are particularly helpful if you find a thimble a bit cumbersome or awkward. There are also small plastic pads available, the size of a 10p coin, which are useful for grabbing a needle and pulling it from a particularly thick or heavily stitched area.

Pounce

Pounce is traditionally made from cuttlefish (white), charcoal (black) or a mixture of the two (grey), and once pounded into a powder, it can be rubbed into holes on tracing paper to transfer a design from paper to fabric. The holes should be made using a small embroidery needle, such as a No. 10 or 9 needle, and spaced about 5mm apart. Once the tracing paper is removed the dots of pounce can be joined together using watercolour, gouache or a fine pen or pencil. A fine drawing pen can give an excellent thin line but colour choice is more limited. Traditionally paint would be used to draw on the design lines rather than a fine pen and the colour of paint can be matched exactly as required, either almost to match the background fabric colour or to match the thread colour. The consistency of the paint should be like that of double cream or tomato ketchup – not so thin or watery that it spreads and bleeds into the fabric but not so thick that it leaves blobs. A thin paintbrush is best to use, to give as fine a line as possible. This pounce and paint method is particularly useful for darker fabrics where the design cannot be seen through the fabric on a lightbox and traced onto the fabric.

CHAPTER 3

BACKGROUNDS

You never realize how much of your background is sewn into the lining of your clothes.

– TOM WOLFE (1930–2018)

Backgrounds are a great way to create perspective and depth, and to draw the eye into the design. They are particularly important within appliqué because by applying one fabric to another we automatically create a background! They can create mood and add colour, texture and relief before any stitching has been worked. Sometimes it is important for backgrounds to be plain and pale in colour so that they sink away and recede, allowing the colours and motifs in the foreground to leap forward and become the focus. At other times the background may need some detail and interest against plainer motifs, to give more depth and distance to the work.

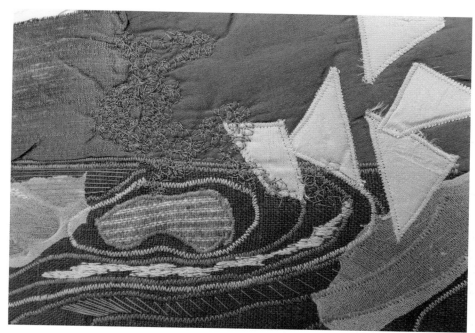

Machine cutwork with applied fabrics including tights, and hand stitching.

OPPOSITE: Rose cushion cover, showing cutwork appliqué background and padded felt applied pieces that form the rose motif.

PAINTED BACKGROUNDS

Backgrounds can be totally flat or raised, depending on what materials and techniques are chosen. Flat backgrounds can be achieved simply by using paints but watercolour pencils, colouring pencils, pens or thicker acrylic paint all work well too. Silk paints can also be used for a more translucent effect and a gutta resist (like that used in batik) can be used to give a firm line or barrier between colours.

Watercolour pencils can be used to keep the design lines quite clear. But if the fabric is painted with water first and then paint applied to the wet fabric, this will

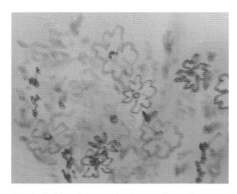

A painted background using watercolour pencils is a subtle way to give interest and detail.

This painted background path with organza on top shows stitching that has been started around the path, which helps draw the eye into the design.

In both these examples leaves have been trapped between fabric and hammered until an impression is left. Worked by Minnie Collingwood, these prints are ideal to use as a background or to embellish.

give more subtle blending and bleeding of colours. For more definite design lines or areas of colour, water doesn't need to be added to the background first but for a smooth transition of colour and pattern, a wet surface can be appropriate to work on.

Flat backgrounds can also use one piece of fabric positioned next to another, as seen in inlay appliqué, usually using felt pieces (explored in Chapter 7). Painted backgrounds can have an added piece of applied organza (or another fine and transparent fabric such as net or organdie,

chiffon or even see-through plastics) that still shows the painted background but adds even more dimension and depth.

Backgrounds can also look effective when the paint is sprayed or splattered over the fabric rather than brushed on with a paintbrush or drawn on with a pencil. This can be a messy business – best done outside or within a box, or on lots of newspaper! It can be helpful to have a big piece of plastic sheeting underneath the fabric being decorated too. A toothbrush gives an effective dotty look that is

best used with thicker paints that will not run. A piece of card or a knife can be used to run along the toothbrush to allow the paint to be released. Spray guns, such as airbrushes, also work well; tape the fabric onto a surface so that it doesn't pop up or move during the process.

Stencils can also be a really effective way to transfer motif shapes onto the fabric; these can be covered with applied fabric motifs over part of the design or over the whole stencil, but can also make up a background onto which more shapes can be added from other fabrics. A stencil is useful when specific shapes are required, rather than a whole pattern over the entire background. Stencils can also be useful to give a shadow effect behind an applied motif. Stiff plastic is usually better to use than cardboard as you can see through it, which helps with placement. Another advantage is that it doesn't go soggy with paint like card may do. Use a sponge or stencil brush that has a round, flat base to apply the paint onto the fabric, using dabbing rather than brushing motions.

DYEING

Fabrics can be totally coloured by immersing them in dye, rather than painting them. This can be useful if threads need to be the same colour as the fabric, as both could be dyed together. It is also useful where a fabric needs to be one colour, rather than painted or shaded in different areas. Another useful technique is to leave parts of the fabric in the dye for longer than other parts to give a shaded or ombré effect. Marbling, tie-dyeing and folding are other ways of decorating the fabric using dye.

Layers of organza can give added depth and be decorated on top as desired, using threads or more three-dimensional elements, such as beads, buttons, etc.

Simple flower shapes from printed Tana lawn are placed under the organza.

Organzas are layered over the padded hill to give a high relief effect and to give some depth to the design.

LAYERING

Shadows and perspective can be created by layering pieces of fine fabrics, such as organza, chiffon or organdie, on top of one another, so that the background remains quite flat but a three-dimensional effect is achieved. A flat background allows for lots of stitching to be added if required, because the layers are thin and still easy to stitch through. This can give a really interesting and sophisticated dimension to the work, especially by varying the amount of embroidery – perhaps more at the bottom and foreground and less towards the back of the design.

TRAPPING MOTIFS

Another effective technique worth trying is to lay motifs or pieces of fabric, such as cut-out flowers or leaves and then trapping them underneath a fine, transparent fabric, such as an organza, before stitching over the top. Bondaweb can be quite useful to hold the chosen motifs in place before laying the organza over the top. And of course then the motifs can be left without any extra stitching around the edge, because they are held in place by the layer of organdie or organza. This can also be a useful method if pieces of old or fragile fabric, such as lace for example, are to be included in the piece. The organza or organdie acts a little like conservation net, protecting what is underneath but not obscuring it from sight.

PADDING

By having more raised areas within the foreground of the piece, the perspective and three-dimensional effect can be even more dramatic and padding is another great way of achieving this. Often padding will be higher near the foreground and become flatter further away, but this is not always essential.

If padding is being added to a central part of the design, cutwork or reverse appliqué can be an effective background to use. Padded areas can be particularly

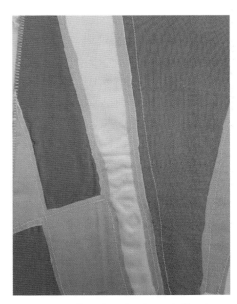

Cutwork appliqué is a simple and effective way to achieve a background. It remains fairly flat, especially where fine and sheer fabrics are used, so that other fabrics or stitches could be easily added on top.

effective, especially where colour is required in blocks, rather than using subtle shading. It can create interest in height and dimension rather than, or in addition to, the use of colour and texture.

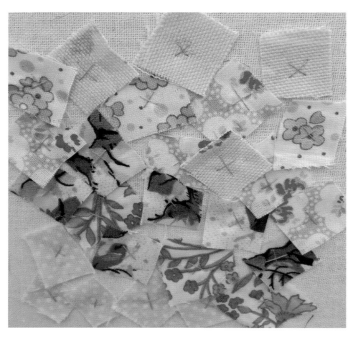

Squares of patterned fabric are held to the background with a cross stitch worked in stranded cotton.

Rectangles of plain silk fabric are held down with groups of long stitches worked in stranded cotton.

Worked by Yvonne Rogers, this example shows the same technique used behind a three-dimensional silk shaded flower.

FABRIC PIECES OR SHAPES

Another effective background for adding texture is to place small pieces of fabric next to each other or overlapping, using small, decorative stitches (for example straight stitches, cross stitches, star stitches or French knots) to hold the fabric pieces in place onto the fabric background. This is sometimes better to do around a motif rather than underneath it, in order to avoid bulk, but this does of course depend on the weight of the fabrics and threads being used and the size and detail of your design.

Any of these examples can be used within different scales and different effects can be achieved depending on whether cotton or silk fabric is used, if stitches use thick or thin threads, if the fabrics overlap or lie next to one another, or if they all face the same direction and are the same shape. Bondaweb wasn't used in these examples, but it could be if a much flatter, still or sleeker effect is required. The Bondaweb would take away any frayed edges as these would get stuck down, so it is useful for neat, precise shapes or pieces but not so good for messy, textured effects.

RIBBONS AND CORDS

Ribbons or cords can also be couched down as part of a border or background within a design. These lines are dense and less subtle than the organzas or layered fabrics so are particularly good for outlines where extra definition is needed or where foreground wants to be exaggerated. Bias binding is also useful as it already has a turned-under edge so slip stitch can be used, which will be totally invisible. This is often used in stained glass appliqué, where bias binding (or ribbon) acts as the lead around the coloured shapes.

A selection of ribbons, lace and braids that can be used.

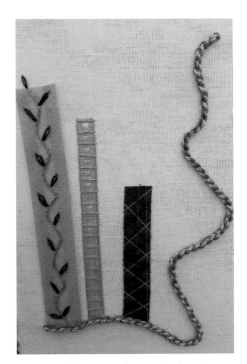

Couched ribbons can be attached to the background fabric using all kinds of stitches: slip stitch and appliqué stitch are good when the stitch doesn't want to be seen; decorative stitches like herringbone or fly can be fun to add interest and texture.

Handmade cords can vary in width, depending how many threads are used in each ply. The top three cords use a mixture of wool, stranded cotton and metallic thread, while the bottom, slightly thicker cord uses just stranded cotton in a mix of shades.

Simply loop the thread around the pencil, hold in one hand and twist in the other until the thread is tightly twisted.

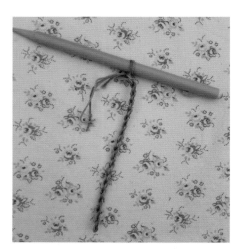

Then double the twist back on itself and let it wind together, teasing it along so that it twists up evenly on itself.

A cord machine has a long handle so that it can be held without getting in the way of the cords. It also has a button which when held down, allows the threads to be twisted individually before letting go of the button and twisting the twists together to make the cord. This can be seen on the picture just behind the top right hook.

Cords give a much higher relief and texture than ribbons, braids and bias bindings, but because they are flat the binding and ribbons can be stitched over and detail added with these decorative stitches. Cords can be useful as an edging or border as well as for use as a decorative texture and can be shop-bought or handmade very easily by using the pencil method described below, or a cord machine.

Using a pencil to make cord is a quick and effective method for simple, fine cords, but a cord machine works well for longer or more complicated cords. There are four hooks to give a 4-ply cord, but they don't all need to be used. Various types of thread can be used but it usually works best to stick to the same sort of thread, so that the tension is even when twisted and pulled tight.

Using a cord machine

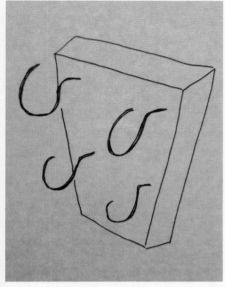

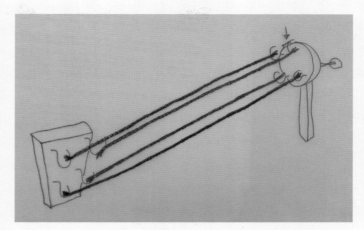

The cords are twisted individually first, by holding the metal square down (see yellow arrow). Turn in the direction to twist the threads rather than untwist them! To check if the number of twists is enough, it can be useful to slacken the twisted threads slightly. If they twist up on each other it has been twisted enough.

The cord machine is held by the black handle and the wood with four hooks attached to it is clamped or tied to a table. Each end holds the thread or threads and can be stretched as far or near as required for the length of cord.

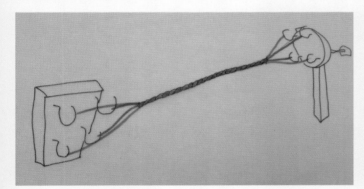

Once the threads are twisted individually they can be twisted together by letting go of the metal square and turning in the same direction as before.

Tie each end before taking off the cord machine at each end. It can be helpful to have an extra pair of hands for this stage! Use a buttonhole thread and tie it around the cord tightly a couple of times to stop it untwisting once it is removed. Do this at either end of the cord before removing from the cord machine.

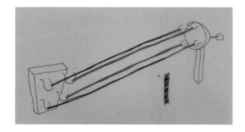

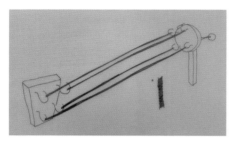

The way the threads are positioned on the hooks will decide the pattern of the cord that is produced.

Machine cords using beads on perlé thread and handmade cord.

The length of thread needs to be cut about four times the length of cord that is required. The lengths can be cut separately or they can be folded in half around the cord machine, depending on the pattern of cord that is required. It is a good idea to just sample a few short lengths in different combinations first to ensure that you have the pattern and thickness of cord that you require. There is no hard and fast rule for how many threads for a given thickness of cord, as each thread will require a different number of strands to give the same width of cord.

Cords can also be made on the machine using the zigzag stitch to stitch over a group of threads. Beads can be added to a reel of thread and added to the threads and stitched over or threads can be stitched over by themselves in thick or thin groups.

These examples all use similar colours, so the machine zigzag and the threads underneath blend together but contrasting colours could also be used for a striped effect on the cord.

Machine cord using a mix of perlé and stranded cotton.

Machine cord using chenille thread gives a more textured cord.

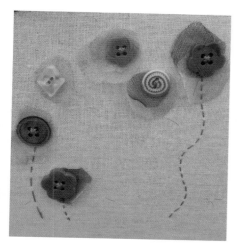

Buttons are stitched over organza circles using a simple running stitch in stranded cotton which gives a flatter, smoother effect than the use of more textured threads, like perlé for example.

Suffolk puffs are used to create some height on an otherwise quite flat appliqué cushion cover and stitches are worked for added texture.

Two pieces of fabric have been layered together, the top layer with heart shapes cut out of it before stitching machine lines over both layers and embellishing around the heart shapes with chain stitch.

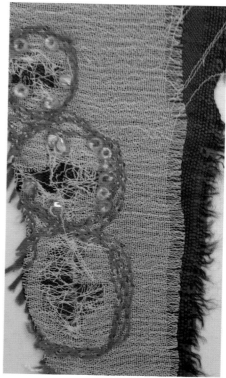

Heart shapes are trapped between silk and chiffon and machine stitched around the edge to encourage them to stand out. Free machine embroidery is added in the background using variegated thread.

BUTTONS AND BEADS

Another idea for backgrounds and borders is to use pieces of fabric (a bit bigger than whatever is going over them) that can be held in place with buttons or beads.

In the example shown, the organza is left with a raw edge; a frayed edge could be used with silk dupion to give a similar effect. A Suffolk puff could be used instead of the organza for a neater, larger and more raised effect, or pieces of felt (which have no fray) could be used. A stitched edge, such as a closed buttonhole or a satin stitch, could be added if a more solid line was required within the background design.

MACHINE EMBROIDERY

Machine stitching, in patterns or randomly, can be a great way to get texture onto a background. It can then be embellished with hand stitching or by adding more fabrics; left by itself it gives finer stitching lines than when hand embroidered. It is also a great, quick and effective way to produce cutwork/reverse appliqué, because the lines can be quickly produced before any cutting is done. Beads can be added for texture, and fabrics, papers or petals can be trapped between layers of fine fabrics to create some depth, pattern and interest.

Flower petals have been trapped between net and organza, and stitched around to hold in place.

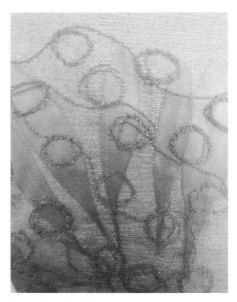

Instead of stitching around each petal, the petals are trapped between silk dupion and organza, and free machine stitching is worked over the top.

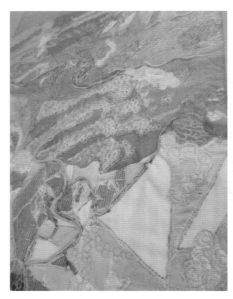

Machine stitching has been used throughout because of the size of the piece of work, to create texture, resulting in almost a fabric collage.

Depending on the colour combinations used, different effects can be achieved. The flower petals are the same but look different in each picture, because of the background colours and fabrics that have been used. Changing the colour of the thread so that it contrasts with the background fabric gives a completely different effect to threads that blend into the fabric, showing off texture more than pattern.

These are just a few ideas for creating backgrounds around or behind a design or motif and some of these techniques can, of course, also be used for the motifs themselves as well as the backgrounds. The main thing to keep in mind is what the background is doing to add to the design. It doesn't want to fight with the main motifs so that the overall image is confused or too busy. Sometimes simply using a patterned fabric as the background can be enough to add interest. In other designs,

it may be that if a small palette of colours has been used throughout a design then layering of fabrics within the background can help to give interest and perspective that just one fabric would just not achieve. Layering of fabrics is also really useful if one is not so confident with paint or where the detail and shading quality of paint is not required. When really intricate or bold motifs are being used, it can be worth cutting them out and just placing them on different coloured and patterned fabrics to see which looks more effective.

It is also worth bearing in mind the colour wheel as these decisions are made: dark tones tend to absorb the light and therefore recede while lighter colours advance to the fore. For example, bright colours like red and orange jump forward while muted greys and blues will sit back and can give depth and distance to a piece of work. Sometimes putting coloured fabrics

together and trying different coloured fabrics on top can help you to choose backgrounds that enhance and show off the applied areas to greater effect.

The Overlord Embroidery, which can be seen at the D-Day Museum in Portsmouth, is a great example of layering of fabrics within background and foreground to create powerful, bold images that paint could not have achieved in the same way. Designed by Sandra Lawrence, it was commissioned in 1968 by Lord Dulverton to commemorate the D-Day invasion of France during the Second World War. It tells the story of Operation Overlord, the code name for the Allied invasion of Normandy in June 1944. It was stitched by members of The Royal School of Needlework and is a wonderful embroidery made from pieces of applied material (some really tiny pieces!) showing various edging and background techniques.

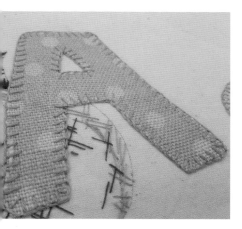

A dark background fabric pushes the paler tones forward.

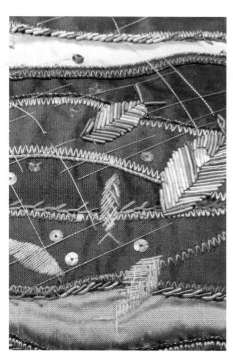

This example shows how simple lines of stitching can create a shape in the background that is not overpowering and does not take over from what is in front.

This stole shows cutwork appliqué in the background in green and blue tones, while the embroidery is worked on top in contrasting colours.

Made of thirty-four panels, together measuring 83 metres in length, the Overlord Embroidery is one of the longest of its kind in the world. Twenty embroiderers worked on the work for five years, using appliqué techniques, cords and some surface stitching.

Many altar frontals use some of these layering techniques and painted backgrounds also, to create perspective without needing any three-dimensional additions which could make the piece too heavy. A wonderful feature of appliqué is that all sorts of fabrics and materials can be used to create foreground and background: laces, sheers such as organza, cottons, silks, plastics, velvet – the list goes on.

It is worth keeping in mind, however, that finer fabrics may work better in a background so that heavier or denser fabrics in the foreground stand out. However, if a design uses all cotton fabrics, for example, then the lighter colours might work better as the background and darker colours towards the front to give perspective. It is important to keep a contrast between what is happening behind and what is in front and layered backgrounds can be really useful for this. As mentioned before, having a play with fabrics at the design stage – laying them on top of each other, laying threads on top of fabrics – can be really helpful in deciding what tones and textures work before applying them to the design.

Once the background is complete, then the order of work can follow the usual pattern: any padding can be applied before any motifs and then once motifs have been added, edges and surface stitching can be used around and on top of the design areas. As with lots of embroidery, the piece is worked background first, working towards the foreground. What is on top is worked last, so it is important to get the background planned and applied before any other fabrics and stitching are worked on top. Sometimes it can be helpful to work a few backgrounds, changing the colours or the fabrics in each one, before deciding which one to use.

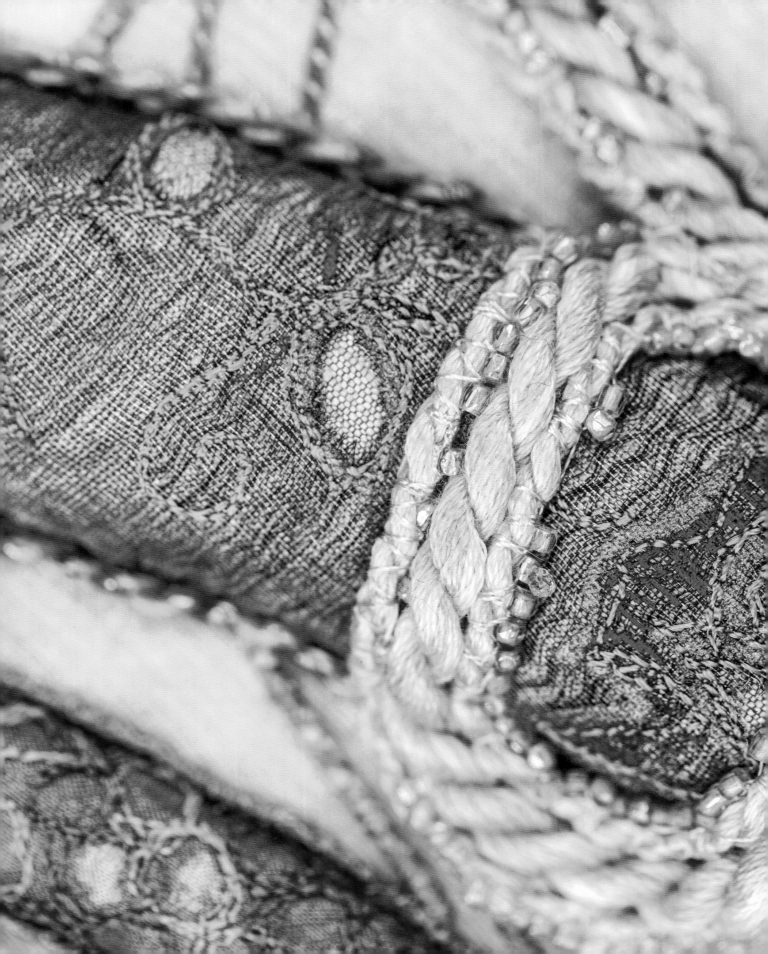

❦ CHAPTER 4 ❦

PADDING

A sense of good design for embroidery does not necessarily depend on the ability to draw; a design for this craft can be thought of in terms of material and stitches. If the work is treated from the beginning as a delightful adventure in textures, stitches, lines and masses, the finished work is almost certain to possess at least one great asset – that of spontaneity.

– KATHLEEN MANN (1937)

There are various types of padding that can be used and lots of these can also be found in other embroidery techniques, especially the carpet and felt paddings, which are used a lot in goldwork and also in more modern raised and stumpwork. Padding gives a three-dimensional aspect to the work and is a particular part of appliqué used to give different levels and heights within one piece of work. It was used in older examples of stumpwork by using up any leftover scraps of fabric or threads bunched together, or sometimes even paper, which would give very intricate small areas of design relief; in appliqué, however, the padding tends to be bigger and bolder. Appliqué shows simpler shapes using smoother padding techniques. Materials such as felt padding, carpet felt or soft toy stuffing are often used.

Starting with the highest form of padding and working to the flattest, a list of most commonly used paddings within appliqué is as follows:

❧ Carpet padding
❧ Felt padding
❧ Soft toy padding
❧ String padding
❧ Vilene
❧ Slip.

A selection of padding materials.

OPPOSITE: This design, taken from a still life, shows padding worked behind the rose and linear sections of the design.

CARPET PADDING

Carpet padding is often used underneath goldwork, usually but not solely used underneath gold leather kid or gold plate, as the carpet felt doesn't then need to be stitched directly into because stitches hold the leather or plate around the edge. Carpet felt gives the highest level of padding and it is (as suggested by its very name) the material that is used as carpet underlay. It needs to be the more traditional, sometimes slightly stratchy, felt padding, rather than the foam version. It is made up of lots of bits of fluff, off-cuts of felt and other materials compressed tightly together to form a thick, stiff felt. It is sometimes backed with foam, which can be removed before use. It can be ordered from many carpet suppliers, and sometimes it is possible to get smaller off-cuts from a local shop.

Carpet felt can be layered up, or just one layer can be used depending on the height of padding that is required. Unlike normal craft felt, when used in padding, the first layer of carpet felt padding needs to be the largest shape and then smaller pieces can be applied on top until the desired height is reached. Each layer needs to be chamfered around the sides; cut at a 45-degree diagonal angle rather than vertical.

Herringbone or long stab stitches can be used to attach each layer to the background fabric. Herringbone stitch is sometimes preferable as it gives a smooth hold that doesn't stitch into and pull the carpet felt. It can be useful to use double thread (such as a Gütermanns polyester thread; any machine thread would be fine) rather than single thread, so that the thread is strong when pulled tightly over the carpet felt. It does not need to be waxed. Herringbone stitches rather than long stab stitches used over the carpet felt give a smoother, neat effect but stab stitches can be used as long as they are long enough.

Once the carpet felt has been applied (as many layers as desired but commonly three) then a layer of normal felt is put on top to cover the rather hairy and scratchy carpet felt. This ensures that none of the hair or fluff escapes into the top layer of fabric. This normal felt layer is applied in the same way as felt padding (see below), using small stab stitches that come out of the background fabric and into the felt by about 2mm or so. The stitches can be placed far apart to hold the felt in position, and then more stitches added about 2mm apart all the way around the shape.

Carpet felt comes in various colours and levels of rough or smooth.

Always chamfer the edges on carpet felt before applying to smooth and round off the edges ready for the top layer of felt to cover smoothly.

Stitching through carpet felt

The carpet felt layer is high, (especially where many layers are used) so it can be best to embroider or embellish the top fabric before it is applied to the felt shape. It can be best to avoid multiple rows of couching or stitching into the carpet felt as it can be tough to get through all the layers and difficult to keep the stitches neat and accurate. Stitches can also pull the padding down so more layers may be needed if lots of stitching is applied afterwards.

Herringbone stitch over carpet felt

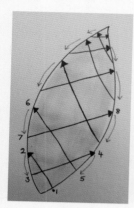

Herringbone stitch is really a form of cross stitch: come up behind where you go down, working up and down each time.

Start with an open herringbone. Make sure the stitches are pulled tightly.

Go back in the opposite direction, filling the gaps.

The second layer, a smaller shape, goes on top. Remember to chamfer the edges, as before.

Herringbone in the same way. Any lumps at the side of the felt can be smoothed down by adding another stitch over the whole shape. This keeps the padding as smooth as possible.

Covering carpet felt with wool or craft felt

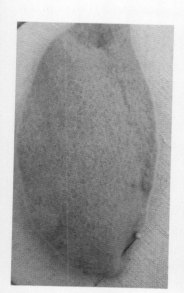

Pin the craft or wool felt in place (or you can tack lightly over the top with herringbone stitches).

Keep the stab stitches open, with good-sized gaps to begin with.

Then go back around the shape, filling in the gaps. This ensures the felt is evenly and smoothly applied.

The finished padded area should be smooth and ready for an edging stitch to be added as required.

This sampler shows the three stages of carpet padding.

The rose has used various layers of carpet padding underneath the fabric, to give maximum height.

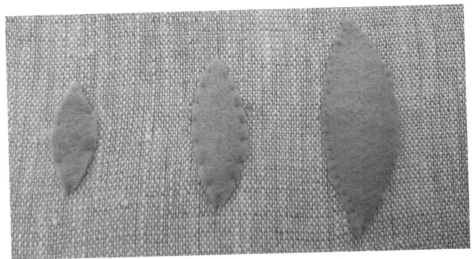

The smallest piece of felt is applied first and the largest last. This ensures a smooth padding effect is achieved. Note how the stitches get closer together on each layer.

FELT PADDING

Felt padding uses normal craft felt and is also very common in goldwork. It is similar to carpet felt padding where many layers can be put on top of each other to create the desired height/padding. Usually up to four layers are used; if more layers are needed to achieve the required height, it would be better to use carpet felt. Instead of working the largest shape first and working to the smallest as in carpet felt, the opposite is worked in felt padding. (The same idea is used in satin stitch padding, where underneath stitches are worked in smaller areas getting bigger towards the edge for each layer until the top layer reaches over all the underneath stitches.)

The first layer of felt padding only needs to be stitched in a few places to hold it in place. Stitches are 2mm in length but can be much wider apart, as seen in the example. The stitches should be worked in single machine thread, coming out of the background fabric and down into the felt shape. (Machine thread is the best choice for stitching down padding because it is stronger than a single strand of stranded cotton and is also slightly finer and less fluffy.)

The subsequent layers of felt can be stitched down in the same way but more stitches may be required as the shapes get bigger. However, it is only the very top, final layer of felt that needs stitches to be about 2mm apart all the way around the shape to ensure that the edge is smooth. Begin with a stitch at either end of the shape to hold the felt in place and then fill in around the shape in between these initial holding stitches. Stitches can be pulled tight to ensure that the felt is smooth and tight. The felt needs to be taut and not baggy, so that it will hold tight any fabric or stitching that goes on top. Stitches that are added to baggy padding will not have a good tension and fabric may look bumpy or wrinkled. It is important that the padding is accurate, smooth and secure before anything else is added. Any colour of felt can be used, usually to match the top fabric so that it doesn't show through dramatically. The thread colour should also match the felt colour.

SOFT TOY PADDING

Soft toy padding can be made from polyester, cotton or Kapok, a natural plant fibre. It is particularly useful when a small section of light padding is required within a design or for a very small area. It is used traditionally in Trapunto quilting, where areas of the design are stuffed by making a small slit in the back fabric and stuff-

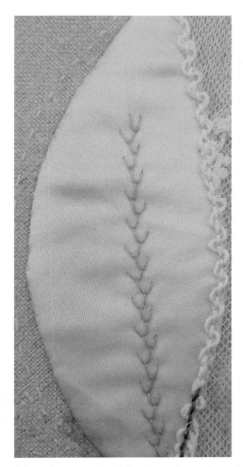

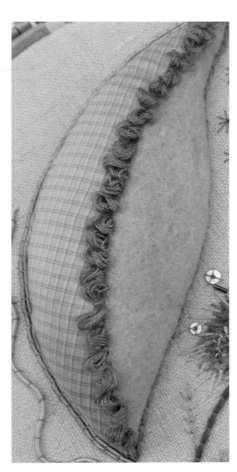

The reverse of the work shows how slits are made in the backing fabric (usually muslin) and stuffed, before oversewing to close.

The front of the work, with padded hearts and flat background.

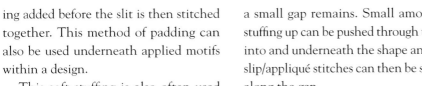

Felt padding can be high or low, depending what effect is required.

ing added before the slit is then stitched together. This method of padding can also be used underneath applied motifs within a design.

This soft stuffing is also often used within raised embroidery for faces and bodies because it can be added slowly until the desired effect is reached. The same method is used for figures as for applied motifs. The motif or shape that is to be stuffed is cut out bigger than required, leaving enough edge to turn under, usually about 4mm but it depends slightly on the size of the motif. Usually one side of the shape is turned under and slip or appliqué stitches are worked along an edge before continuing around the shape until

a small gap remains. Small amounts of stuffing up can be pushed through this gap into and underneath the shape and small slip/appliqué stitches can then be stitched along the gap.

STRING PADDING

String padding can be useful for texture and pattern underneath threads or fabric. A variety of string can be used, depending on the effect and pattern required. Within goldwork, white string and a soft yellow string (much like a perlé thread but without the twist) are the common

choices. These are stitched down, much like couched threads, and cut away underneath if the shape gets narrower, much like the technique we use when working trailing too (see Chapter 7).

Stitching into soft padding

Soft stuffing is not really suitable to be stitched into unless it is extremely tightly packed into the shape. Otherwise stitches may distort the padding and flatten it too much. It is best to work any decoration first before applying the fabric and then stuffing.

It can be helpful to cut small stitches into the turned-under edge to give a smoother finish, especially where there are curves or corners; alternatively, gather the fabric with a small running stitch. This is also a useful technique when applying a slip.

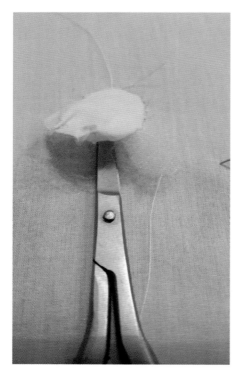

A small pair of scissors, a tapestry needle or small wooden stick from a paper quilling set can be useful to push the soft stuffing into the shape. A laying tool, such as a mellor, can also be helpful for slightly bigger shapes while a cocktail stick may be useful for small shapes, to push the stuffing into the corners without making holes in the fabric!

Within appliqué, however, a wider scope is available, depending on the required effect. Threads can be twisted together and covered, piping can be made, and thick or thin string can be couched over leaving different widths of space or

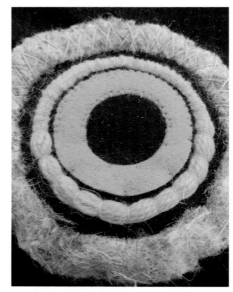

String padding can be a useful base to lay fabrics over, shown here between felt and carpet padding.

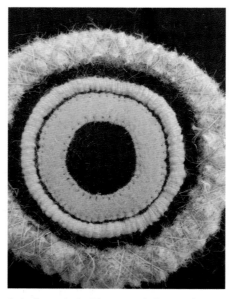

As before, start with open stitches, and then repeat the couching stitch around the shape, going in between the stitches/gaps.

gaps between each couched line to give different patterns.

The most commonly used string padding techniques outside goldwork are found in Italian *trapunto* or Provençal *boutis* quilts. Both techniques use a similar double line of stitching (either running or double running stitch) to create a channel that is filled. Italian quilting uses a soft wadding string that can be threaded through a big needle whereas *boutis* uses stiffer cotton, a mixture between a crochet wool and a soft string. The idea is that the pattern is padded from behind, much like *trapunto* but in a long, thin line rather than motif shapes.

The main idea of string padding is that it can be used for narrow, long shapes that would be difficult to pad with felt without the felt shredding or breaking. Cord could also be used instead of string padding and left to show rather than being covered. It is also a good method to use if the applied fabric needs some underneath texture, perhaps for a tree trunk or the roof of a house.

Italian quilting (*trapunto*) uses a channel to create a raised pattern.

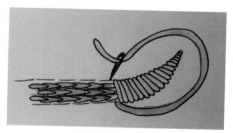

Split stitches come up in the first stitch and down halfway along and keep repeating. Because each stitch lies half on top of the previous stitch it gives immediate padding, although stitches can also be worked again on top of one another for higher relief still.

The fabric can be attached to the Vilene either by gluing the fabric to the back of the Vilene (a heavyweight Vilene is needed for this), or, preferably, by stitching from one side of the turned-under fabric to the other. Just make sure the thread is not pulled too tight or it will distort the shape.

SPLIT STITCH PADDING

This is also useful for small areas and can be done in slightly finer string or thread, such as a *coton à broder*. This padding is usually used underneath satin stitch but can be used under felt or fabric too in small areas, such as those used in the Overlord Embroidery perhaps.

VILENE

As mentioned in the materials list, Vilene is a useful substitute for cardboard really. It is a stiff material, much like craft felt really but much denser and doesn't bend or pull apart. It is much hardier and more durable. It come in white and various weights are available and it is really useful to wrap fabric around and then attach to the background or piece of work as if it were a piece of fabric with a turned edge.

Vilene is particularly useful where fabric is thin and turned-under edges would show through if no Vilene or felt was used. The good thing about Vilene over felt is that it has a much harder edge to work against. It is also useful for small applied pieces or motifs such as a vase

– wired flowers could be used and then the wire covered by the Vilene vase; because the Vilene is thick and dense the wires would not show through. Or a wall within a design could be cut out of Vilene and covered with fabric, already painted to look like stones or bricks. This could then be applied on top of hills or along the bottom of a design hiding any frayed edges of previously applied fabrics. It is not so good for really small, intricate shapes as the fabric has to turn over and around each part of the Vilene.

SLIPS

A slip is anything that is worked, decorated or embroidered off the frame and then cut out and attached to the background fabric. It can be a face, as already mentioned, which then gets stuffed with toy stuffing once on the frame, but a slip does not usually need stuffing. Slips are often seen in raised work, not only as faces but also as hillocks or flowers perhaps. A Suffolk puff that is made and then applied could be called a slip.

A piece of canvas that is stitched, say in tent stitch, can then be cut out leaving

Stitch a small running stitch around the canvas, a couple of millimetres outside the stitched area. Use a machine thread, doubled in the needle. Pull the running stitches to gather the canvas or fabric and push the excess canvas underneath, using small appliqué or slip stitch to attach to the background. Keep these small and even so that the slip edge is smooth.

1–2cm space (depending on size of slip) and applied in the same way as a face; small running stitches to gather the edges in and turned under before applying to the background with small slip or appliqué stitches.

CHAPTER 5

EDGES

Although the threads of my life have often seemed knotted, I know, by faith,
that on the other side of the embroidery there is a crown.

– CORRIE TEN BOOM (1892–1983)

Once a fabric motif has been applied to a background fabric, there are many possibilities of how to finish and edge this applied area. This is important to do when the stab stitches that are holding down the applied motif to the background need to be covered, if you don't wish them to be seen within the design.

There are a few general points to bear in mind before edging stitches are worked along the fabrics.

✻ Always knot on the front and work two stab stitches close to the knot. These can be stitched over with your chosen stitch.

✻ Finish in the same way, with two tiny stab stitches before bringing the thread to the front and cutting flush against the fabric.

✻ Always work stab stitches along the applied fabric before edging, using a machine thread or one strand of stranded cotton in the same colour as the fabric being applied.

✻ Keep thread lengths wrist to elbow length; this helps to prevent the thread from twisting, becoming fluffy and wearing thin.

✻ Use a No. 12 embroidery needle for the stab stitches if possible as the fine needle will make it easier to get through thicker fabrics; you will also avoid marking finer fabrics or causing extra, unwanted fraying.

✻ Always come up in the background fabric and down into the applied fabric.

✻ It can help to begin in the middle of the motif and then keep stitches fairly wide apart (2–3cm); once around the shape, go back and fill in the gaps so that the stab stitches are about 2mm apart around the entire shape. This will help keep the edge smooth and in position.

Fabric can also be applied with a turned-under edge, which again does not need anything added or any stab stitches used first. Otherwise, a fabric will usually be applied by the use of small stab stitches and these will usually need covering. These stab stitches would usually be worked in the same colour thread as the applied fabric so that they blend in well and they should only be 2mm or so in length so that it is not necessary to use a thick stitched line to cover the stab stitches, unless the design requires it.

Decisions about the type of edging stitch can be made at the design stage. Applied fabrics in the foreground may need higher, denser edging stitches, while motifs that are fading away into the background may require more open, lighter stitching around their edges. Also, heavier fabrics may need heavier edging stitches such as a line of cord, couching or trailing while lighter fabrics with a motif that is very smooth perhaps, may just need a satin stitch or long and short edge in the same colour as the fabric – or perhaps just a turned-under edge. Although these decisions may be made at the planning stage, they can also be changed or adapted once

OPPOSITE: Monkey design, using frayed, couched, long and short, and buttonhole edges.

Small stab stitches ensure the fabric is firmly secured to the background and can be easily covered with a variety of edging stitches.

Sometimes fabric motifs are applied with a frayed or raw edge and simply attached with a running or double stitch and need no further attention. No stab stitches are necessary.

Stab stitches on easily fraying fabric

Sometimes if a very light or very heavy fabric such as an organza or an upholstery fabric or velvet has been applied, the stab stitches may need to be longer to ensure that the fabric does not fray away from the stitching.

the piece comes together, in order to make shapes and motifs stand out more clearly, for example.

The most commonly used edges in appliqué are described in the list below. Frayed and turned-under edges (as mentioned earlier) are not stab stitched to the background fabric first and therefore do not require extra stitching after the fabric has been applied, unless further decoration is required to add to the effect.

Turned-under edge is a neat technique to use if no further texture or stitch is necessary to enhance the design or where a smooth, crisp edge is required.

Various edges are chosen here to complement and add to the overall effect of the piece.

FRAYED EDGE

Thinner fabrics (which can be layered on top of one another) work particularly well for frayed edges. It is a very useful edge when a hard line is not required and can be built up by using layers of fabric, not necessarily all the same colour. If a round shape is required, such as a sun or the middle of a flower then layers of frayed fabric can be more effective to give the circular shape, rather than trying to create frays in a circular direction. The choice of fabric has to be carefully thought about as some cottons and heavy fabrics do not fray easily. Of course the length of the fray can be short or long depending what effect is required. For fringing on a carpet or a mane on a lion, long frayed threads would work well while feathers on a bird might need a shorter frayed edge.

Frayed edges work best without the use of Bondaweb so that the fabric can be pulled apart and frayed to the desired effect. Silk dupion works particularly well because the threads pull out easily without breaking.

Frayed edges can be applied by the use of a running or backstitch along the fabric or another more decorative or less uniform stitch – such as open long and short stitch – can be effective and follow the frayed lines nicely. Care has to be taken in order not to catch or pull the frayed edge underneath the stitches. A variety of threads can be used in the needle: stranded cottons and machine thread are probably best, as anything thicker like a perlé or *coton à broder* might just be too heavy against the weight of fabric and particularly the frayed edges.

The monkey's head uses frayed fabrics, which are only stitched at the base in order to keep the feeling of movement.

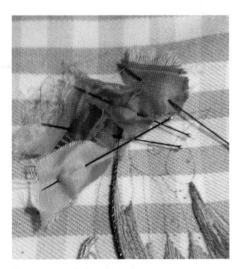

The cockerel's head has been given a feathery look by the use of frayed fabrics, first pinned in place using fine ento pins.

The fabric has been attached using backstitch in a matching colour of stranded cotton.

TURNED-UNDER EDGE

A turned-under edge, as described earlier, gives a neat and precise line. It is useful for garments and hill edges or where a design includes simple pattern and shape, for example, a pop-art type design or a background of hills or shapes that has added stitches on top but doesn't need the 'busy' appearance of edging stitches as well. Remember to work a turned-under edge on a tight (not slack) frame, otherwise once completed and pulled tight the appliqué/slip stitches will show.

When working a turned-under edge the fabric motif needs to be cut out bigger than the original to allow a turn under of about 5–10mm. It may be that only one side of the motif has a turned-under edge, in which case the other side can be cut flush with the tracing paper pattern.

Bear in mind that if the fabric you have chosen is thin or light in colour, it is a good idea to cut out a piece of similar

A simple design shows off the turned edge along just the bottom of the design.

coloured felt (or Vilene) using the tracing paper pattern as a guide. The fabric can then be turned around the felt and caught down with small overstitches coming out of the fabric and catching the felt along the turned under side, before then being attached to the background fabric.

Once the edge is turned under the felt (or if no felt is necessary) then the edge can sometimes be ironed under (if the edge is straight) or it can be pushed under gently and fine pins used to hold it in place.

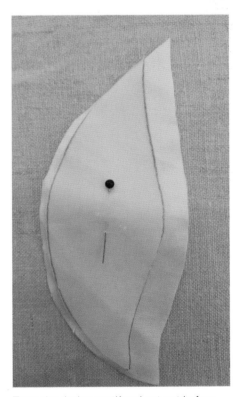

Trace the design motif and cut out before placing onto chosen fabric, keeping in mind which way you want the grain line to go. If the shape is cut on the bias remember the fabric will stretch, which may make it harder to lay flat.

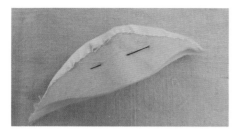

Felt underneath the fabric will prevent the turned-under edge from showing through the fabric once it is applied.

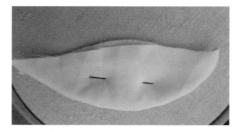

A fine entomology (ento) or lace pin is used to attach the fabric to the felt while the edge is turned around the felt and stitched to attach. A fine pin is essential to avoid making marks in the fabric.

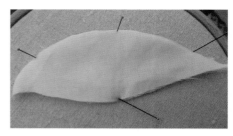

It is important to just pin where necessary to hold in place as this stops the fabric puckering and to place the pins in the crease of the fabric rather than through the top.

It can be helpful to tack the motif shape using herringbone stitches to hold the shape to the background fabric and avoid pin holes, or simply to avoid catching on the pins as you are stitching.

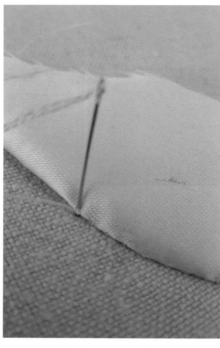

This stitch is known as an appliqué stitch or slip stitch, and the idea is that it is invisible. It is also used in quilting appliqué for the same reason: it doesn't show but pulls the applied motif tightly down onto the background with a smooth, turned-under edge, so that it can sometimes be difficult to tell if the motif has been applied or printed onto the fabric.

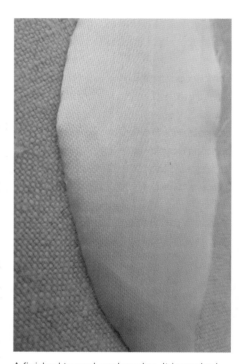

A finished turned-under edge. It is worked along one side of the leaf while stab stitches hold down the opposite side, ready to be covered with feather stitch, once the lace has been added.

Size of stitches

It is important to keep these stitches small and tight, and spaced about 3–5mm apart depending on the size of the motif. If the edge is straight, stitches can be slightly further apart but if a tight curve is required, small close stitches will be needed to give a smooth, even line.

Once the motif is in place, using Gütermanns polyester thread or a machine cotton (a length of stranded thread would be a bit thick and fluffy, and not quite strong enough), come out of the background fabric close to the turned edge and then down through the edge of the turned-under fabric.

This process illustrates the importance in planning an order of work, so that you know the order in which the various edges need to be completed. It is often best to complete a turned-under edge before any other edges, otherwise it can be difficult to get to it and turn the fabric under easily.

COUCHED EDGE

A couched edge is a really useful way to neaten an edge that may be a bit jagged. Fabric that is a bit thick and bumpy can be finished off nicely with a couched edge, when smooth stitching such as satin might still show a ridge between applied fabric and background.

Couched edges are very versatile because they can use any thread. Some ideas are listed below but really anything can be used for the core thread(s).

Metal threads
These are commonly used in gold and metalwork.

Gimp
Gimp is similar to some metal threads, in that it has a core of threads, which is wrapped in silk thread rather than gold or metal thread.

Stranded cottons
Separating each strand and putting them back together again ensures that the strands sit smoothly and closely together. Use a minimum of six strands and as many as required depending on the thickness of the line required.

Perlé
Because of its twist and weight, perlé is useful when texture and thickness are required.

Wool
This gives a softer, thicker texture than stranded cottons.

This leaf sampler shows various types of couching, using a variety of threads, including wool, stranded cottons and gimp to create different effects over flat and padded applied leaves.

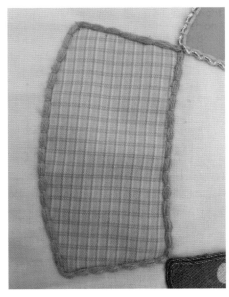

Couched stranded cotton gives a smooth line, much like gimp.

A selection of metal threads. They come in a variety of colours and textures, either as a core of thread with metal wire or paper wrapped around the core, or as metal coiled.

Gimp comes in all sorts of colours and different thicknesses.

A more puffy couched edge is achieved when using wool.

Chenille can also give a softer line when couching, while chainette lies flat.

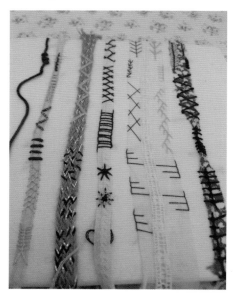

Sampler shows various types of braid and ribbon couched down with stranded cotton.

Chainette or chenille

These threads, which can be tricky to thread through a needle, can give a good texture or sheen to an edge. Often they come space dyed, which can be fun and add some depth.

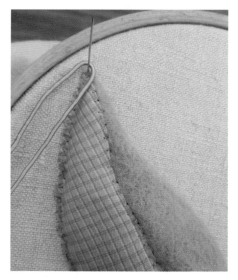

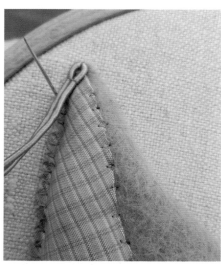

It is not always necessary to plunge both ends of the couched line. When using a double row of gimp or metal thread, or if you divide the thread in half and double it/ bend it round itself, the end can be stitched instead of plunged.

Ribbons, ropes and strings

Offering a range of alternative textures, these can add dimension to a piece of work.

Usually it is most effective when couching to use a finer thread to couch the core than the same thickness as the core, as this can look clumpy and messy. However, it does of course depend on the effect required.

When couching one line made of several strands of cotton, the angle of the needle needs to angle out from the line and then angle in towards the line so that the couched thread is pinched. This will encourage a rounded edge rather than a flattened out pile of threads.

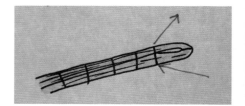

Couch as if stitching over only one line, but be careful not to angle too acutely or the double row of thread may become squashed together or overlap.

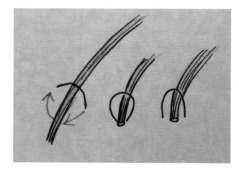

This drawing shows the shape of the thread around the couched strands when couching one line. This encourages the couched line to puff and sit proud rather than flat and wide.

Couching a plant stem or single line

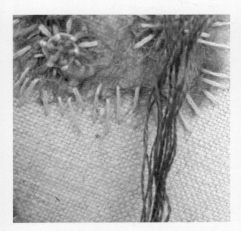

Couching is used here along a stem line rather than against an applied motif edge. Two small stab stitches are made along the line of the couching to start the thread; come out just below the start of the line.

Come up on one side of the line. (When couching over a motif edge come up on the background fabric right next to the motif.)

Come down on the other side of the line or down onto the motif fabric, making sure the stab stitches are covered. Your needle should angle down towards the line or where the fabrics meet.

Using a No. 20 chenille needle, thread the core and take through (plunge) to the back of the fabric. Do the same on either end.

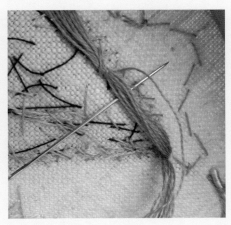

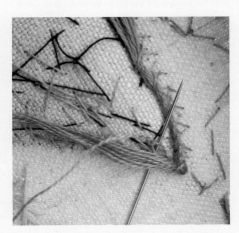

Tie back the ends on the reverse of the work by overstitching and catching a little of the fabric with each stitch. You can use the thread that was used to stitch over the couched line if there is some remaining or use a new thread. Just make sure the couched thread is oversewn about 2cm before cutting and always stitch this plunged thread back underneath the couched line.

Cut away any excess thread.

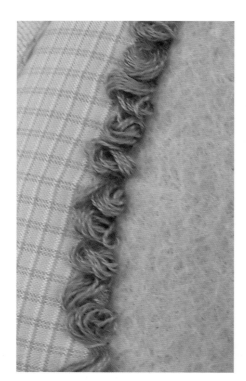

Looped couching is stitched where the applied silk meets the background fabric. Here ten strands of cotton are couched over with one strand of cotton, using a No. 10 or 12 embroidery needle.

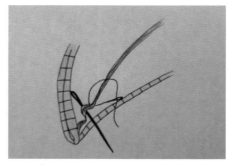

Looped couching is much easier to do on a frame as one hand is needed to hold the tapestry needle to make the loop, while the other hand pulls down the couching stitch.

Smooth trailing is worked in stranded cotton because it gives a smooth, shiny finish.

Usually trailing creates a very smooth line, but again it can be given a looped effect much like couching, by simply leaving a gap between groups of couched stitches.

LOOPED COUCHING

Looped couching is very similar to smooth couching as the stitches are spaced 3–4mm apart and any thread can be used depending what effect is required. For a softer, more blousy effect wool can be a good choice while stiffer threads such as string or gimp will give a more upright, strict effect.

It can be a useful edge to use where a wider area needs to be covered, for example over thicker or more fraying fabrics where the stab stitches might have to be longer.

The thread(s) being couched are attached, to begin, with an overstitch a couple of mm away from where the line will be plunged. The next couching stitch is worked 3–4mm away depending on the size of the motif and before that stitch is pulled tight, lay a biggish tapestry needle (No. 22/20) underneath the thread being couched over and lift the thread upwards until desired loop size and pull the couching thread tight. Repeat for each loop until the end, when both ends of the couched thread can be plunged to the back and tied back as before.

TRAILING

Trailing is a form of couching but instead of leaving a gap between each couching stitch, these stitches are couched right next door to each other with no gap – much like one would stitch a satin stitch. It is often found in broderie anglaise white-work and also in raised stumpwork, but can be used in various other embroidery techniques too. Again the couched, core thread(s) can be anything from *coton à broder* thread to wools, varying in thickness/number of threads used to create this core, depending on how thick a trailing line is required.

Traditionally trailing can be worked in *coton à broder* or stranded cotton, for both core and couching over. Stranded cotton will give a smoother finish when stitched as a single strand to couch while a *coton à broder* will show each individual couched stitch more obviously. *Ver à soie* thread is a good silk alternative to stranded cotton for the couching, but has more bounce in the thread, so might be better to avoid in the core threads and use only for the couching. It is also more expensive than stranded cotton because it is silk, so might be wasteful to use in the core thread, since it is just going to be covered! Perlé thread works less well for smooth trailing but can be fine for the core where a thicker line is required. Wool behaves itself well for trailing as, like stranded cotton, the strands sit close to each other and squash together to form a smooth core as well. Usually one would stick to the same thread in core and couching but this is not always absolutely necessary.

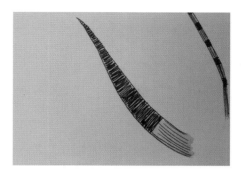

Wool trailing, from thick to thin, creates a softer and lower level of trailing. Remember to cut away the underneath core threads, leaving the top and sides, for a smooth result.

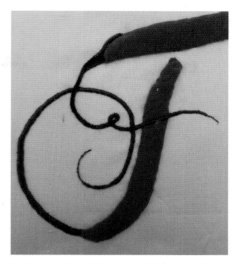

Trailing can be all the same thickness or it can vary from thick to thin, as the design requires. This trailing line started as twenty-four strands of cotton, narrowing to just eight strands.

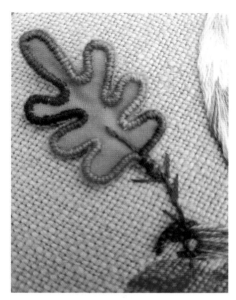

Smooth shading can be effective for a soft effect, while block changes of colour can match the pattern in a fabric.

When using stranded cotton as the core, it is advisable to use at least six strands or the trailing can become a bit weedy! Usually more strands are needed than one expects. Remember that because the couching stitches are so close together and tight, these will pull the core threads together too, making them narrower than before.

It is important to start at the widest part of the trailing and finish at the narrowest part, as you do not want to be adding in threads to the core but only taking them out from underneath, leaving the top and side strands to give a smooth and even trailing, once couched over.

Trailing can be shaded or left as one colour, depending what effect is desired. When the couched thread does change from one shade to another it is important to blend shades, unless a stripy effect is deliberately required. To shade subtly it is usually best to have two needles on the go at the same time so that the colours can be gradually changed. When one colour has been used, simply bring it up to the front, on the design line, a couple of centimetres away from the couching. When the colour is needed again, simply make a small stab stitch along the design line to pull the thread back to the core.

METAL THREADS

A huge range of metal threads is available, in an assortment of colours, thicknesses and textures. They can be couched down along an edge using exactly the same method as described above. The only difference is that the couched thread should be waxed so that it doesn't break or become fluffy; usually one strand of stranded cotton or a polyester Gütermanns thread is used to couch over the metal threads.

Core thickness

A good way of checking the thickness of your core threads is to simply twist the strands together in the hand to see what thickness these threads will make once couched over.

Using two or more needles

Working more than one colour thread, and more than one needle at a time always bring your needle to the front of the frame, rather than leaving it underneath, so that it doesn't get tangled when introducing another needle and thread.

Couching metal threads

When couching metal threads, it is helpful to come up on the outside edge and down into the fabric and the inside edge. Not only is it better to go down into the applied fabric but it should give the neatest edge coming up out of the background outer edge of the motif; also, if the couching stitch is a bit big or long it won't show so much on the inside edge.

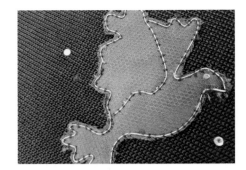

Couching worked over thin wire.

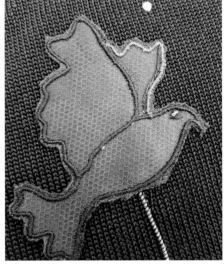

Trailing worked over the same design.

Leaf sampler showing a variety of gold threads couched down to cover edges of applied silk fabric leaves. Where metal threads have a core of thread they are plunged, but a pearl purl metal thread that does not have a thread core can simply be cut.

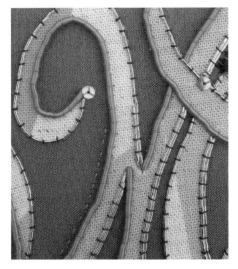

Couching over Japanese thread.

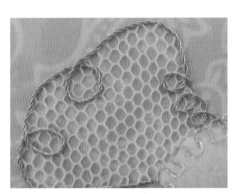

Stitching through twist.

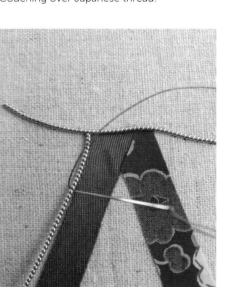

Stitching over pearl purl.

Poppies by Dee Jackson, showing couched edges.

Detail of handmade cords used in the rose appliqué. These are thick and thin depending which area they are edging and whether they are against padded motifs or not.

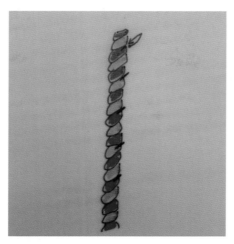

Stitching down cords so that the stitches are invisible is achieved by stitching out of the background fabric and down in between the ply twists of the cord. The angle of the stitch follows the angle of the twist or cord.

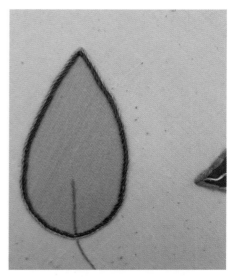

The green twist (or cord) is stitched first from either side. Then the gold is stitched from the outside edge towards the green twist but not between the twists. This ensures they butt up close to one another without a gap.

CORD

As described in Chapter 3, cord can be bought or handmade to suit the design. Thickness can also vary depending on the size of the motif and edge being covered. Cords give a rounded, higher edge than couching, with more texture. They can be solid in colour or shaded and variegated.

Cords can be made out of any thread; stranded cotton works well for fine, smooth cords, while perlé and variegated twisted threads can add texture. Wool can also be used but does have a different pull to cotton so can be challenging (but not impossible!) when used together. Metal fibres or threads can also be added to a group of cotton threads and twisted together to good effect. Shaded cords can work well to connect to fabrics that sit

next to one another, perhaps two green hills or two leaves of different colours, which overlap one another. Meanwhile textured cords can add dimension and depth, for example if used on the trunk of a tree. It is helpful to bear in mind that cords do sit proud and will not sink into a design in the same way as decorative and flat stitches, such as satin and long and short stitch. Cords are particularly effective on padded areas that need something heavier than a flat stitch, which might be in danger of disappearing.

It can be helpful to stitch down a cord from both sides if it is worked with no other stitching on either side. But if it is sitting next to or butting up against another couched line, it is easiest to stitch the cord down along the outside edge, not the edge against a stitched or couched line.

Stitching a cord against or on top of an applied area of fabric

Come up on the motif line and down into the loop of cord, between the twists.

Down through the twist.

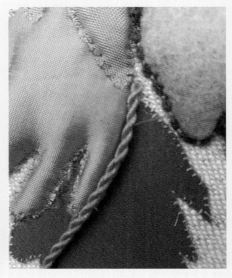

Up into the background fabric, a couple of twists away from the last stitch.

Always put a stitch at a turn or corner, and perhaps one at either side instead of missing a couple of twists, to ensure it sits tight. A small stab stitch in the fabric also helps to hold stitches steady.

Plunge the end of the cord using a lasso or big chenille needle and tie off at the back. If the cord is particularly thick you may want to untwist the cord and plunge it in sections, one at a time.

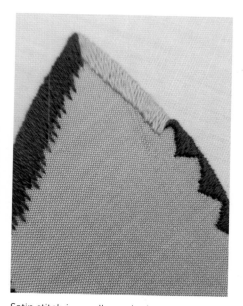

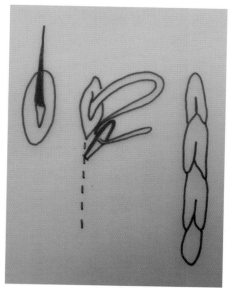

Satin stitch is usually worked over a split stitch edge that runs next to the edge of the applied motif along the background fabric. Stitches are usually the same length but can vary, more like a long and short stitch, or form a pattern like this triangular one.

Split stitch.

SATIN STITCH

So far the edges that we have looked at have been mostly couched, apart from our frayed edges. All of these couched edges are high and often but not always higher than the applied motif. We now look at some of the other commonly used edging stitches that give a flatter, smooth appearance and are particularly suited to flat applied motifs. This isn't to say that they cannot be used on padded motifs as well of course, but they do particularly suit fabrics that lie flush with one another.

Satin stitch is used a lot in broderie perse appliqué and lots of other embroidery techniques. It is one of the harder stitches to master particularly because it can be hard to keep the angle consistent, as much as because the stitches need to be smooth and evenly stitched. Tension and placing is important for this stitch and therefore it is usually worked over a split stitch edge.

PADDED SATIN STITCH

Padded satin stitch edges also give a smooth effect, but add depth and height within a design. Split stitch is worked in the same way as before, around the edges. There are two ways of then padding the area before working a satin stitch over the top but whichever padding stitch is used it is always kept within the split stitch. It is only the top layer of satin stitch that goes over the split stitch, hiding it from sight.

Laid padding looks very like a satin stitch, also worked within the split stitches. The only difference from satin stitch is that these stitches do not have a long stitch at the back. This is because the back does not need padding and also because the front stitches do not need to be held down smoothly by a long stitch behind them, because they are going to be covered by the satin stitch and not seen.

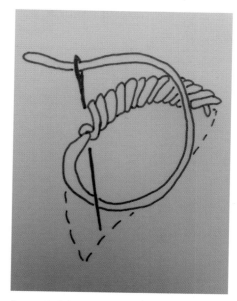

Rope stitch looks very like satin stitch but is worked in one go, rather than working a split stitch first.

Stages of satin stitch

  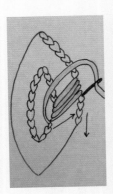   

Split stitch around the outside edge of a motif. This needs to be as small as possible so that it doesn't move or distort when stitching is worked over the top and against it.

When satin stitch is required to be the same length, becoming a smooth, even band of stitching, a second inside split stitch can be helpful.

Start in the centre to get the angle of stitch. Working a diagonal line rather than a horizontal can make it easier to work.

The angle of stitch should be opposite to the direction of travel. This will help keep the angle from slipping.

Once one side is filled, work the other end, coming up the opposite side and down the opposite side to before.

The angles on a satin stitch edge can vary within the same shape, depending on the effect required.

Split stitch padding

Laid padding

  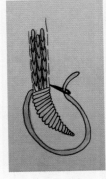   

Split stitch padding is particularly useful for narrow shapes, such as edges or lettering.

Split stitch padding can be worked in long or short stitches that come up in the middle of each other to form lines of padding. They can also be stitched on top of one another if more height is required.

A final layer of satin stitch goes over all the padding and split stitch.

Work the split stitch and one layer of padding within the area.

Add a second layer of padding in the opposite direction to first layer.

Top layer of satin stitch, over the split stitch in the opposite direction to the final layer of padding. Working in the opposite direction ensures that the stitches sit on top of one another rather than sinking in.

This blue flower shows the feathery nature of long and short stitch. Stitches are of different lengths in a random arrangement: not just long or short but also lengths in between.

This flower, however, has been worked in Appletons crewel wool and follows one direction. It is possible to see the rows of long and short as each row is worked in a different colour, but because the stitches vary in length the rows are still disguised enough to give a smooth effect.

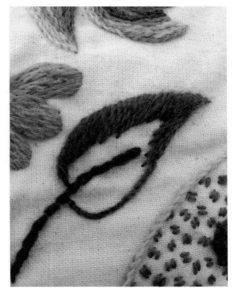

The leaf next to the flower has been worked in only one row, much like an edge is worked against any applied motif. The split stitch remains on the bottom edge but has been covered over with long and short stitch everywhere else on the leaf.

LONG AND SHORT STITCH

Long and short stitch is also known as silk shading and in some books may be referred to as 'thread painting'. The idea is that it covers sometimes large areas just with stitch and that the rows of stitch, where one stitch meets another, are disguised, making it unclear where each stitch finishes and begins so that it creates a smooth, shaded impression much like painting would do.

However, when using long and short as an edge with applied fabric, it is only necessary to use one row of long and short stitch.

It is usual to edge the shape to be stitched first with a split stitch. These stitches should be worked in a colour of the long and short stitch or where various shades are used, the split stitch should be worked in the middle shade. Split stitches need to be as small as possible, so that the line of split stitch does not move but stays rigid and firm. The long and short stitches will be worked over the split stitch and push against it to give a smooth edge so it is important that these stitches are firm!

It is not always absolutely necessary to use split stitch underneath the long and short stitch if a feathery or more uneven edge is required. Also the split stitch does raise the height of the long and short slightly and this is not always desired. If a thick fabric has been applied, sometimes this edge is enough to stitch the long and short against without the need for a split stitch. As a general rule, however, it is advisable to use split stitch, usually with the same thickness of thread as being used for the long and short stitch.

Satin stitch worked with a split stitch along just the outside edge gives the satin stitch more of a long and short stitched look, with stitches showing a slightly uneven edge as there is no inside split stitch line.

Long and short stitch with a split stitch border

Outline of motif to be worked in long and short stitch.

Work the split stitch around the edge of the motif, keeping stitches as tiny as possible.

Drawing of long and short stitch, showing varying lengths. Angle of stitch is important, so just as in satin stitch, start towards the centre where it is easier to see the angle clearly.

Stitches should be worked close together, one after the other but not overlapping. If stitches are worked with gaps between which are then filled in, the result can look bumpy instead of smooth.

Finished motif in long and short stitch.

This button shows a flower motif that has an open, spaced out long and short stitch with no split stitch required because of the more feathery, open edge that is required.

BUTTONHOLE STITCH

Buttonhole stitch is a very traditional way of applying an edge to a raw fabric motif. It is sometimes confused with blanket stitch, which has a slightly squarer looking stitch. Either can be used but buttonhole is the name more frequently used within embroidery.

It is not always easy to tell the difference between the stitches but buttonhole stitch has a top edge of stitches from bottom right to top left while blanket stitch has stitches that go from bottom left to top right. Buttonhole tends to look neater and uses less thread. It is also often used in broderie perse appliqué and also on quilts. Most books do not show the working of blanket and buttonhole as different but some practitioners state that the needle is pointed in different directions for each stitch: pointing towards the motif for buttonhole and away for blanket. Others state that blanket is simply a more open stitch, worked often along the edge of a fabric (like a blanket), while buttonhole is closed, as it would be when actually stitching a buttonhole for a button on a shirt. Anything more open than this becomes a blanket stitch. What is certain is that both do the same job! The main thing to remember if choosing to use a buttonhole stitch for the edge of a motif is that the

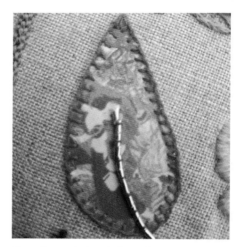

Open buttonhole stitch worked over a leaf motif.

shape of the motif needs to be simple; if it is too jagged or small and detailed, the buttonhole can look messy and untidy.

Buttonhole stitch can be worked over a split stitch or a running stitch, but isn't really necessary unless it is being worked as a buttonhole against an edge that is being cut away. The edge of the button-

A closed buttonhole stitch is worked over small stab stitches in one strand of cotton.

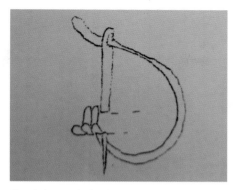

Simple buttonhole stitch can be worked open or closed, depending on the desired effect. Start with an 'L' shape but mirrored so that it faces the left (if you are right-handed; leave as it is written if you are left-handed) and come up in the loop to continue. Buttonhole is worked over the tiny stab stitches on a tight frame. Buttonhole can follow the angle of the motif being stitched, usually following the same angle as the stab stitches.

Simple open zigzag is effective on this stole as a background within cutwork appliqué.

hole just needs to be against the outside edge of the fabric motif, with the stitches going down into the fabric and the needle coming up, out of the loop against the edge of the fabric. This also pushes the applied fabric down instead of coming up out of the applied fabric, which can distort or encourage it to move and lift.

MACHINE EDGE

Using a sewing machine to attach one piece of fabric to another is a quick and strong way to create an interesting background, especially useful for landscapes. It works best for larger motifs and longer edges as the smallest size of zigzag still needs to be tall enough to attach the fabrics together. Like buttonhole and really most sorts of appliqué, it works best with simple, uncomplicated shapes.

Usually a zigzag setting is used to create an open zigzag or a more closed zigzag which gives a smoother impression, like that of satin stitch. However, other decorative machine stitches can be used, as shown in Rosie's sample, to give a more open or intricate detail to the work.

Machine edge is particularly useful for backgrounds. Rosie McKellar's appliqué uses this technique most effectively within the sea background.

Straight stitch can also be used where a frayed edge is required, or when using felt (which doesn't fray so the edge doesn't need to be covered). When using any of the machine stitches it is not usually necessary to turn under the fabric, but if a thin fabric (like a cotton or silk dupion) is being used then the fabric could be turned under to allow a more open zigzag to be worked on top without any danger of fraying. For anything heavier it is best not to turn the fabric under as this can just make everything a bit too bulky, especially if it is for a background.

Jackie Thompson's simple teacup design uses edges of closed machine zigzag stitch, using metallic and matt machine thread to great effect.

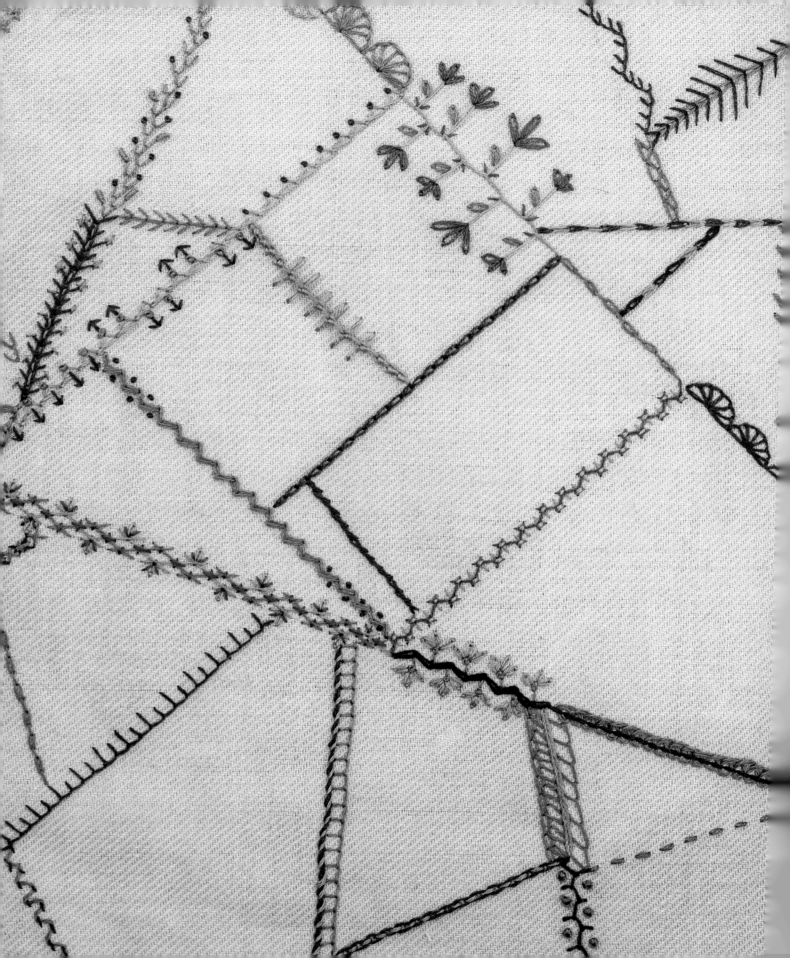

❧ CHAPTER 6 ❧

STITCHES ON EDGE

Take your needle, my child, and work at your pattern; it will come out a rose by and by. Life is like that
– one stitch at a time taken patiently and the pattern will come out all right like the embroidery.

– OLIVER WENDELL HOLMES SENIOR (1809–94)

As well as the standard edging stitches described in the last chapter, there are of course lots of other embroidery stitches that can be used to great effect along the edges or on top of an applied shape or motif.

STRAIGHT EMBROIDERY STITCHES

All basic embroidery stitches can be used in appliqué of course. French knots and bullions work well to create a textured edge, while stem stitch or chain stitch can be used with varying thicknesses of thread to create wider bands of stitch; these can be used as a foundation on which to add further elements, as shown in some of the examples in this chapter. Whipping, wrapping and weaving through stitches all adds decoration and impact, as does adding other stitches to existing ones.

Running stitch

A simple line, usually straight, which is used to attach fabric together, as an outline or as a hem. It is also used for quilting, and is particularly prominent in Kantha quilting, when two fabrics are attached together by rows of running stitch without any wadding in between.

Double running stitch looks like a row of backstitch but is worked by going back into the gaps left by the original running stitch. It is useful when a heavy line of double stitching is not wanted on the back of the work.

Simple running stitch can be worked big or small, with any thread you choose.

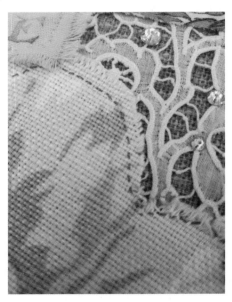

Small running stitches.

OPPOSITE: Blue sampler of edging stitches.

Running stitch is worked next to a chain stitch for added decoration.

A double row of running stitch.

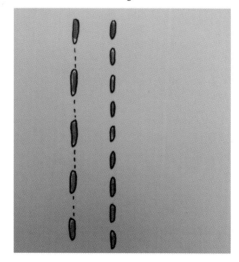

Perhaps the simplest stitch – made up of simple dashes – but perhaps the hardest to keep even.

Backstitch can also be worked in various sizes and threads.

Backstitch

Unlike running stitch, which has gaps between each stitch, backstitch creates one continuous line of stitching. Double running stitch creates the same solid line, but does not have as much stitching on the back of the work, like backstitch does, because it works back to the previous stitch rather than forward.

In stem stitch, the direction of the stitch goes from bottom left to top right. If the angle is the opposite – i.e. bottom right to top left – then the stitch becomes outline, not stem. Outline is similar to stem stitch, but looks more twisted and cord-like.

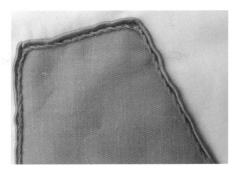

Stem stitch worked inside a row of gimp.

Stem stitch worked within the centre of a motif, leaving fabric edges unattached.

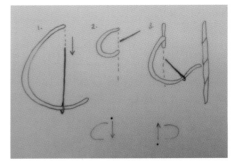

It is important which side of the stitch the loop sits on, so that the stitch is worked correctly.

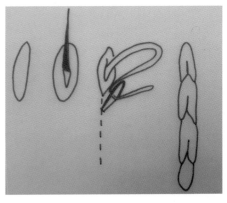

Split stitch has multiple uses, partly because it is a firm stitch and can be worked in different ways.

Stem stitch

Stem stitch is often seen on lettering and as an outline to other stitches, such as trellis. It is also useful as an edge, when a fine line is required rather than a fancy or decorative one.

Remember the word 'up-right' when working stem stitch. The loop goes on the right when working up, away from yourself, and the loop goes on the left when working down, towards yourself.

Split stitch

Split stitch looks a little like a small chain stitch. It is useful for shapes with sharp points but also as a line over which to stitch long and short, and satin stitch to give a smooth edge to those stitches. The stitches need to be as neat and tiny as possible, as although they won't be visible, the smaller the stitches, the less likely they are to move around. They need to be firm so that the stitches over them sit smoothly

and make a smooth edge. Split stitch was also used on the Opus Anglicanum embroideries for the faces. By using the stitch in a circular motion, around and around, firstly in the cheeks but over the entire face, shading would naturally occur just from the direction that the stitching was worked in. Split stitch is also used for padding, underneath narrow and long shapes and for lettering.

Chain stitch

Chain can be worked simply by itself, but there are many variations to it as well. It can be used as an outline or as a filling stitch worked in rows next to one another. By changing the thread and size this will change the look of the stitch too.

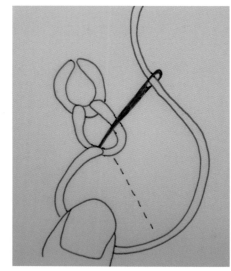

Chain stitch has many variations and many uses.

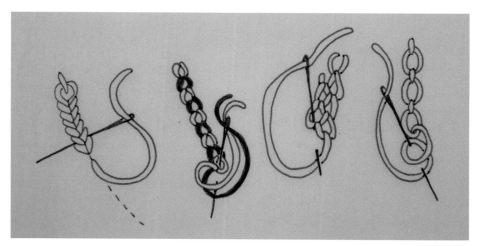

Variations of chain stitch include (from left to right on the picture): heavy, chequered, double and cable.

DECORATIVE EMBROIDERY STITCHES

Embroidery and surface stitches that can be used for edges of appliqué shapes and motifs are many, and only some of them are included in the following list; many have variations and additions to change and develop them even further, depending on the effect that is desired – simple or much more complicated and decorative.

Fly stitch

Useful for attaching two fabrics together, this is a pretty stitch that can be used for feathers and edges. Fly stitch can be worked open or closed, big or small depending on the effect required and the size of the space to fill.

Large and open fly stitch.

Small and shaded.

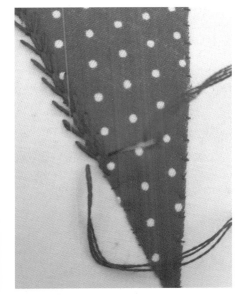

Fly stitch in progress.

Fly stitch in wool.

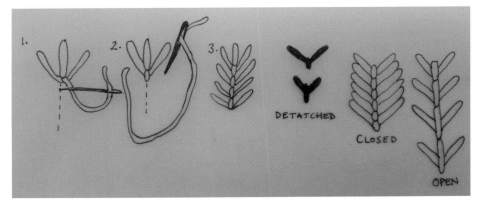

Step-by-step drawing of fly stitch.

Feather stitch

Another pretty stitch that can be worked single, double or triple, depending on the width of stitch required.

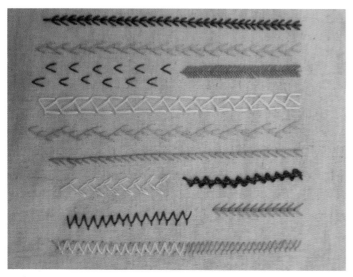

Stitched sample showing a variety of single, detached, closed, open and other variations of fly and feather stitches.

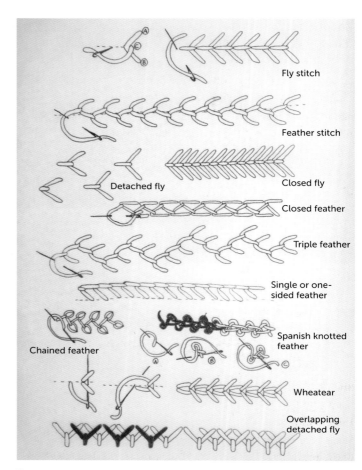

Fly stitch

Feather stitch

Detached fly

Closed fly

Closed feather

Triple feather

Single or one-sided feather

Chained feather

Spanish knotted feather

Wheatear

Overlapping detached fly

Explanations of stitched sample, showing how fly and feather stitches can be used in many different ways, to fill different spaces and patterns.

Single feather stitch worked in stranded cotton.

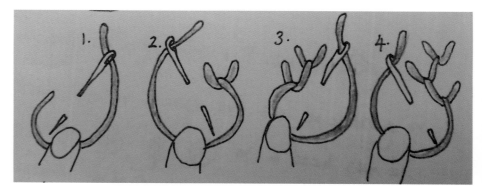

Step-by-step drawing of feather stitch.

Decorative buttonhole stitch

This looks a bit like blanket stitch, and is often used for edging felt to felt on soft toys or felt baby booties etc. and of course in appliqué, more often flat fabric to fabric or felt to felt. It is probably more effective when worked in perlé or *coton à broder* thread, rather than a flat cotton stranded, as the twisted thread gives some height and roundness to the stitch. However, the sample shows all the stitches worked in stranded cotton which does work fine too.

Single buttonhole stitch can be worked open or close together, depending on what is being edged or covered. If a raw edge needed totally hiding then a closed buttonhole would work better, but on felt or a turned edge open would look pretty and be just as effective to hold the fabric together. Just make sure the stitches still hide the small stab stitches used originally to apply the fabric to the background.

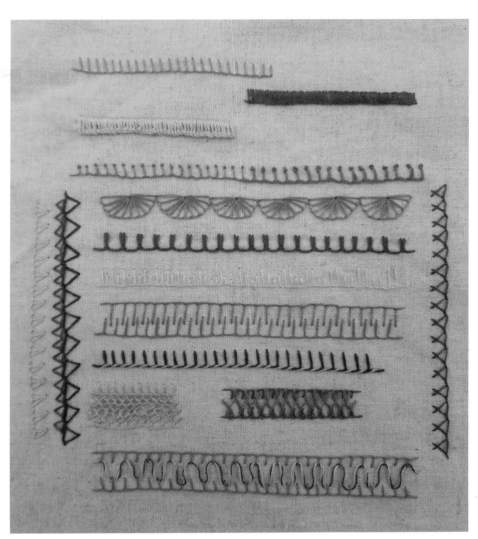

Buttonhole sampler worked in one, two and three strands of stranded cotton.

Thread choice

For higher, more textured, open stitching use a perlé twisted thread or a *coton à broder*; for flatter, close and smooth stitching, use stranded cotton.

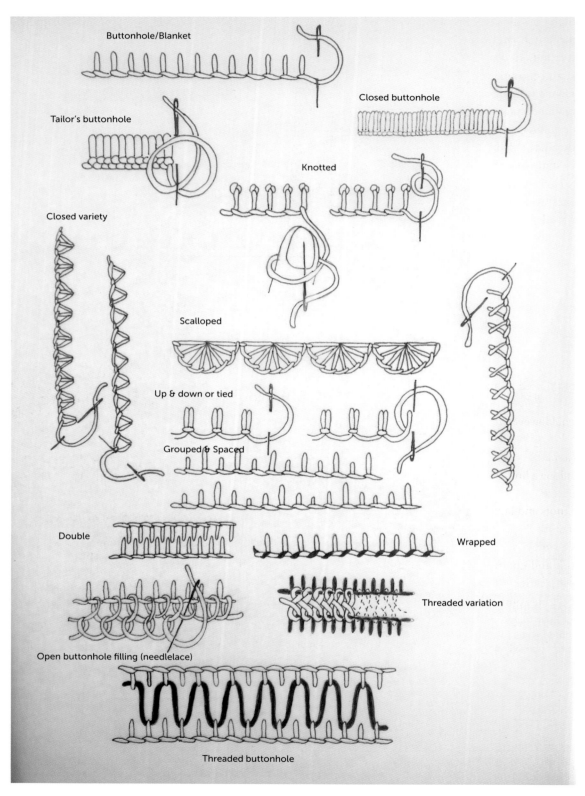

Buttonhole/Blanket

Tailor's buttonhole

Closed buttonhole

Knotted

Closed variety

Scalloped

Up & down or tied

Grouped & Spaced

Double

Wrapped

Threaded variation

Open buttonhole filling (needlelace)

Threaded buttonhole

Explanation of sampler stitches shows how many variations within the same stitch are available, to create very different effects from the same origin.

Vandyke stitch

This is often put together in the same group as Cretan, fly and closed herringbone, as these stitches all work well within small leaf shapes. Giving an impression of vein lines, they can be worked open or closed, but are equally useful along a straight line or as detached shapes.

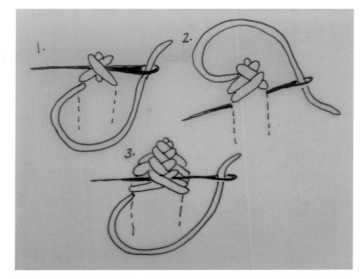

Vandyke stitch. This has a much higher plait effect through the middle of the stitch, while Cretan is a flatter stitch, but still has that similar central twist pattern.

Herringbone

As we have seen, this is often used as a hemming or mounting stitch – a practical rather than decorative stitch. However, it is very useful as a cross stitch to join two fabrics together and also as a smooth close stitch within leaf shapes or along a line. It is very versatile and can be added to with smaller stitches or French knots and lazy daisies to decorate it further.

Herringbone stitch along with others, such as running, backstitch and chain stitch, can all be added to with lots of other stitches so that it becomes quite unrecognizable. Lazy daisies (also known as detached chain) are wonderful to add to a row of stitching to give a more indistinct line. French knots and simple straight stitches can also create interesting and imaginative new patterns and cross and star stitches can create height and texture. These variations can be seen on crazy patchwork quilts but could be happily adopted within an appliqué piece, perhaps on the edge of an applied hill or the skirt of a dress.

Herringbone stitch can be worked big and small, close together or far apart, and interlaced with contrasting thread or other stitches to give a variety of stitch.

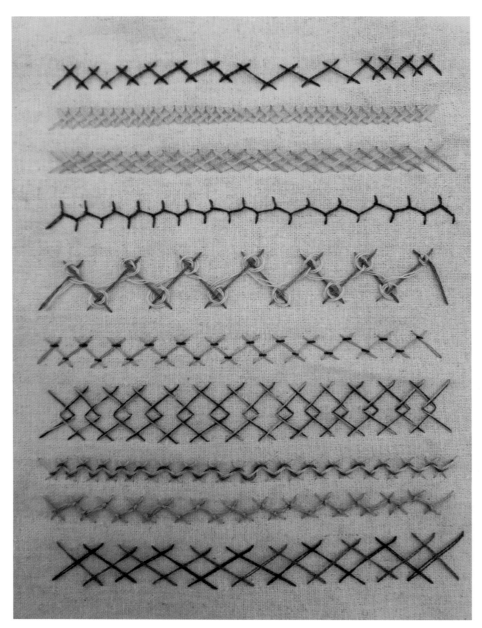

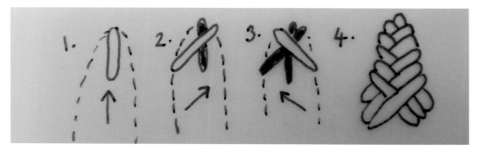

Trellis can be used to stitch over paper or fabric, a little like herringbone but more like a filling stitch.

The sampler has been worked in stranded cottons but would look very effective worked in perlé and variegated threads as well.

Closed herringbone step-by-step.

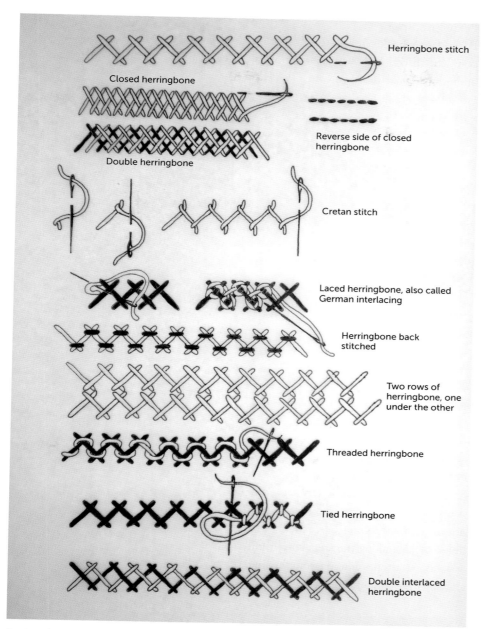

Herringbone stitch

Closed herringbone

Reverse side of closed herringbone

Double herringbone

Cretan stitch

Laced herringbone, also called German interlacing

Herringbone back stitched

Two rows of herringbone, one under the other

Threaded herringbone

Tied herringbone

Double interlaced herringbone

Explanation of sampler stitches showing how diverse each stitch can be.

Chevron stitch

This looks a little like herringbone without the cross; a zigzag stitch that works well to create a straight edge.

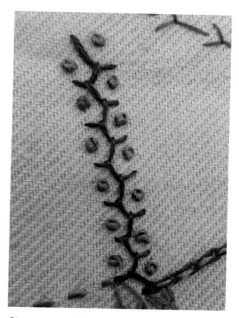

Chevron used along an edge looks rather like a herringbone. Added French knots can give a more decorative look.

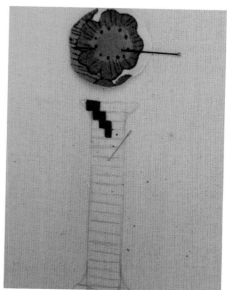

A slightly different stitch, also called chevron (in crewelwork), but worked more like a burden stitch or block shading. Blocks of five satin stitch make up a zigzag pattern much like a Florentine effect.

Threaded backstitch

As previously mentioned, these simple line stitches can be effective by themselves but can work wonderfully as a foundation on which to weave and add further stitches, to create pattern and to hide an edge.

Pekinese stitch

Based on a backstitch, a contrasting coloured thread is woven through and around the backstitch to create a looped effect, very similar to that on a threaded backstitch.

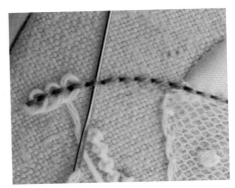

Pekinese stitch is worked on a backstitch and then threaded back on itself to form loops.

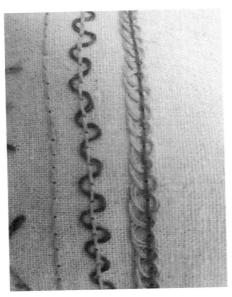

Single backstitch, woven.

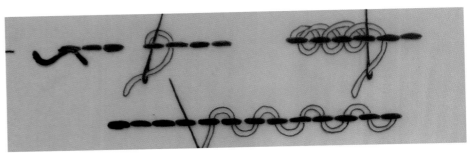

Pekinese and woven backstitch step-by-step.

Petal stitch

Based on a stem stitch and a lazy daisy, this stitch combines the two in an unbroken line. It is a more decorative stitch, but still hides an edge along the stem stitch line and looped stitches coming from the line create pattern and interest.

Threaded backstitch is just a backstitch that is threaded with a contrasting colour. It can give an effective stitch that covers an edge successfully, shown here double.

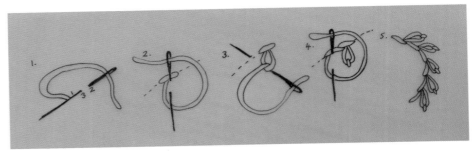

Petal stitch worked in about four stages as a continuous line of stitch.

Knotted and raised embroidery stitches

French knots

French knots can be worked along a line or edge or they can be worked separately or together as a group. They create wonderful texture and height, especially when worked in thicker threads. Make sure the needle you use is not too small or it can be tricky to slide the twist off the needle! Only one twist around the needle makes a French knot. For a bigger French knot, use thicker thread in the needle.

Bullion knots

Bullion knots are another way to create texture; they can be particularly effective worked next to one another, a little like one would work purls in cutwork on goldwork. They are also useful as flower petals and within edges and motifs. Bullions can be as fine or heavy as required, depending on the thickness of thread.

French knots can be used within a design on a motif.

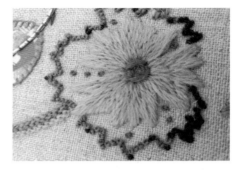

French knots worked around the edge of a motif, to create interest and dimension.

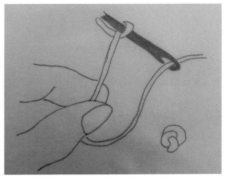

Always make just one twist around the needle.

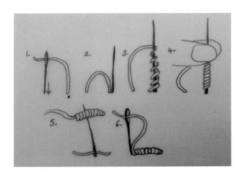

1. Decide on the length and make a stitch this length in the fabric but leave a loop instead of pulling the thread all the way down to form the stitch.
2. Come back up in the same place the stitch was started.
3. Holding half the needle under the fabric, twist the loop of thread around the needle, adding a couple of extra twists to give a slightly more generous, curved bullion.
4. Twist your finger and thumb back and forth to release the twists as you pull the needle out, twisting all the time.
5. Take the needle under the bullion and tease the twists towards the fabric.
6. Go back down in the same hole or as close to it as possible, where the thread came from originally.

Bullion knots (the dark green leaves in this example) add height to an applied motif.

Needle size

When choosing which needle to use, these stitches are going to need a sharp point – either chenille or more likely an embroidery needle, because it is longer in length. The size should be big enough that the thread is fairly easy to put through the eye of the needle and pull through the fabric, but small enough that it doesn't leave a big hole!

Portuguese stem stitch is most effective when a thicker thread is used.

Portuguese stem

Portuguese stem stitch and coral stitch are stitches that both give a knotted effect. Portuguese is also used a lot in Mountmellick embroidery because it gives a height and texture to the work.

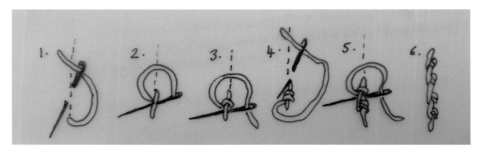

Portuguese stitch step-by-step.

The size or length of the first stitch in the Palestrina knot determines if the stitch has 'arms' coming out from the knots. A small stitch will give knots only while a longer stitch gives lines of thread either side of the knot.

Palestrina knot

The Palestrina knot is stitched along a line, working towards you. It begins with a slanted stitch onto which the thread is wrapped under and through to create a row of knots, with or without stitches at either side of each knot. It works best with slightly thicker thread as this makes the knots more prominent.

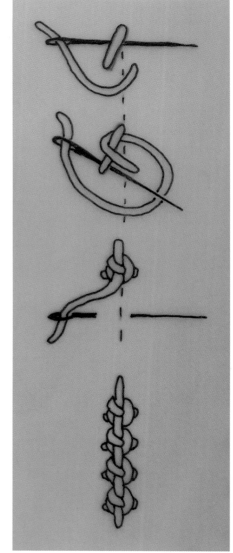

Palestrina knot is really formed of three basic moves, before it starts again.

Coral stitch

This stitch is a bit like a row of French knots on a line. It is made by 'stepping over' the thread with the needle before coming back up into the loop. Again, this stitch is more effective with a slightly thicker thread as the knot will become more prominent and raised.

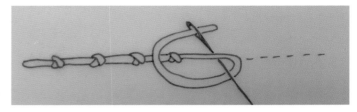

Coral stitch. Always keep the thread taut when working, which will ensure the knot is tight and firm.

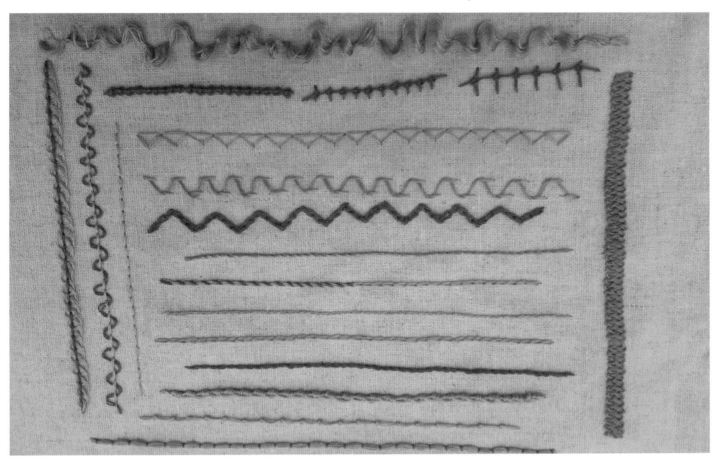

This sampler demonstrates lines of stitching, including more knotted stitches such as braid, Palestrina, Portuguese and coral.

Cable plait stitch

Cable plait stitch is another stitch used in Mountmellick embroidery and also used with gold or fine metal thread to give the effect of a gold braid on banners and ecclesiastical pieces.

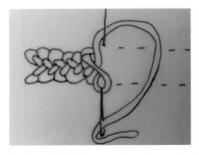

Cable plait stitch is most easily worked by drawing two lines a small distance apart, to stitch against. This keeps the width of the stitch even.

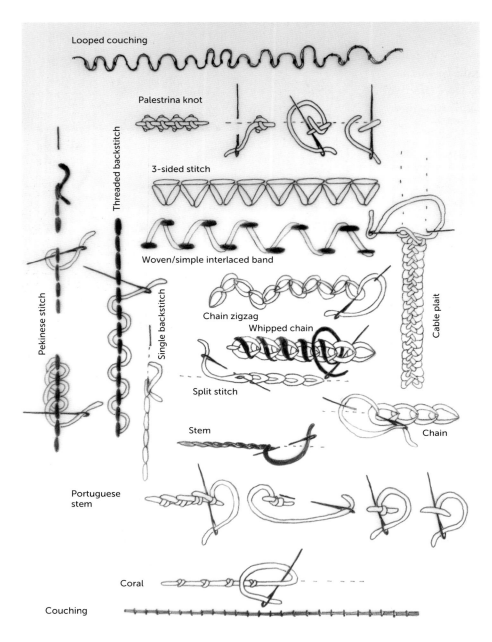

Looped couching

Palestrina knot

Threaded backstitch

3-sided stitch

Woven/simple interlaced band

Pekinese stitch

Single backstitch

Chain zigzag

Whipped chain

Split stitch

Cable plait

Stem

Chain

Portuguese stem

Coral

Couching

Explanation of sampler shows how adding to a stitch can change its effect, simply by whipping or changing direction of the stitch to give a new look.

Beads, buttons and ribbons

Buttons and beads can be a great addition to an edge, creating height, shine and shimmer. Small round beads can be more delicate while wooden or painted beads can add strong pattern and depth to the work. Adding ribbon can enhance textures, and it is useful for hiding any unsightly edges. Be careful to choose these additions so that they complement the design and don't take over from other details.

CRAZY PATCHWORK

Many of the embroidery stitches described above are also seen in crazy patchwork and some of the Victorian examples are wonderful in their combination of not only different stitches but also fabrics that they use: velvets, cottons and silks all mixed together with a huge variety of stitches in perlé threads, cottons, metals and silks.

Often, crazy patchwork also has motifs embroidered and applied on top of the patchwork and it can be as busy and as full of pattern and stitch as possible. Originally made to use up old pieces of fabric, offcuts from a dress or a pair of curtains might be used which is why they have such a variety of fabrics within them. They often tell a story and can be very personal, perhaps including a wedding dress fabric or an embroidered motif or family crest.

It can be difficult to see all the various stitches included along the edges of each patch because of all the pattern and imagery that goes onto these quilts. Beads and buttons are often added along with applied braids and ribbons. The busy texture and flamboyance of these quilts is not for everyone but the ideas and materials

The name 'crazy patchwork' comes from the amazing variety of fabrics and threads used.

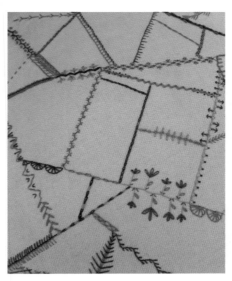

Some of these stitches used in crazy patchworks are shown here, on a plain piece of linen, in order to see the stitches more clearly. Although in this example they have not been used against an edge of fabric, they can be used as edging stitches to great success.

This vintage dressing gown is made entirely of crazy patchwork pieces, but the seams have not yet been decorated with edging stitches.

Small or large, contrasting or blending in, adding three-dimensional objects like beads or pleated ribbon can be highly effective, especially if the button contrasts with the fabric.

Applying fabrics for crazy patchwork

Fabrics are usually applied to a calico or cotton base, turning under any top edges using a slip or appliqué stitch, so that frayed edges do not show through the embroidery stitches. Any edges that are covered by braid or ribbon can be left as a raw edge.

Attaching beads and buttons

Make sure that thread is matched either to the bead or to the background fabric so that stitches blend in. Machine or fine silk thread tends to be stronger and finer than stranded cotton for this purpose.

they contain can be an excellent source of inspiration.

Embroidery stitches used for edges along applied fabric shapes or motifs can use a variety of threads: perlé, *coton à broder*, silk or stranded cottons. Most of the examples shown use either Anchor or DMC stranded cottons: two or three strands in a No. 10 embroidery needle is usually about right. The *ver à soie* silk threads are a very similar stranded thread to use, where silk rather than cotton is desired, as it handles in much the same way as stranded cotton but gives a greater shine.

CHAPTER 7

OTHER APPLIQUÉ TECHNIQUES

*I love taking prints, embroidery, appliqués – precious things that seem to be from
another time, and using them to create a contemporary, new story.*

– ALESSANDRO MICHELE (B. 1972)

There are lots of variations of appliqué and many different materials to use. This book has aimed to cover the main techniques for embroidery appliqué, touching on some of the other ideas that can be included under this umbrella; this chapter explores some of these variations. Some of the techniques described below use stitches that have already been explored, such as couching on transfer appliqué, and buttonhole, satin and turned-under edge in broderie perse appliqué. But the effect can be very different because of the way each technique uses the stitches or combines them with particular fabrics or within a particular design.

TRANSFER METHOD

This method of appliqué is often used when the embroidery needs to be transferred onto a new backing fabric. Often

it is used in ecclesiastical embroidered pieces such as an altar frontal or a stole, where the embroidery is still in good condition but the backing fabric (often silk, which degrades faster than other fabrics) has started to tear, fade or become weak from sunlight or just overuse. It is a really valuable way of making sure that the embroidery has a long life and can be enjoyed and used for as long as possible.

1. Often before the embroidery is cut out, a tracing will be taken first to ensure placement is correct on the new backing.
2. The embroidery is then cut out from the backing, very carefully, leaving about 3mm around the edge, using small, sharp scissors and being careful not to catch the embroidery!

A bird from an old piece of fabric has been cut out and applied to a new background. Stranded cotton has been couched to hide the raw edge.

OPPOSITE: Example of broderie perse: chintz motifs on linen using buttonhole and satin stitch edges.

109

3. The backing fabric (often a linen or silk) can be framed up onto a slate frame but left slack before tacking stitches are worked on either side of the embroidered motif, to hold the embroidery in the correct place onto the new backing. The tracing paper pattern can be placed onto the motif just to check it is all in the right position before any stitching is started. Lace pins can also be used with the tacking stitches but only where needed, to avoid any unnecessary pin marks.

4. Small stab stitches, much like those used to apply felt padding (or other applied fabrics that are being edged) are used around the edge of the embroidery, using a machine thread (polyester or cotton or a fine silk thread depending on what the background fabric is made of). Stitches should usually be about 3–4mm apart, worked by coming out of the background fabric and down in between the embroidery a couple of millimetres. A No. 12 embroidery needle is best – because of its fineness it will not damage the embroidery –

but a No. 10 is also fine for slightly thicker threads.

5. Stranded cotton is then usually used to couch over the stab stitches, hiding these and the edge of the cut line. Usually the stranded cotton is chosen in the same colour as the background fabric so that it blends in. The number of strands used depends on the area being covered but usually no fewer than six or eight strands are used, with just one strand to stitch over the threads being couched.

SHADOW WORK

Shadow work uses a herringbone stitch to create pattern and fill motif spaces, and a pin stitch to attach fabric to the wrong side of cotton organdie so that it shows through the organdie to the front.

It can be the same colour and fabric as the organdie, traditionally white thread on white fabric, or it could be a completely different colour organdie or fabric to the thread colour, as long as the herringbone stitch can be seen and that the fabric being applied is not too much heavier than the organdie base. Paper can also be used to good effect for more decorative pieces that

are not being used or washed, and cotton Tana lawn, such as a Liberty print, can be used to create lovely patterns and colour. Organdie can also be painted or dyed to create more contemporary effects or subtle backgrounds.

A backstitch is worked along two perpendicular lines, stitching alternately from top to bottom line which causes a herringbone stitch to develop on the underneath side of the cotton organdie. It can be

Shadow work sample shows applied fabric and herringbone stitch on sheer cotton organdie fabric, worked with one strand of stranded cotton, and then made into covered buttons.

A lavender bag decorated with herringbone stitch and Liberty print Tana lawn fabric is added using pin stitch.

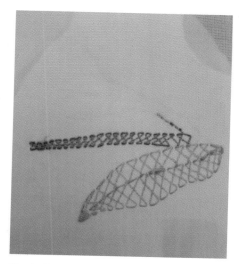

Herringbone and pin stitch make up the basis for shadow work and once mastered, more detailed and intricate patterns and motifs can be designed and worked.

An antique example of Italian shadow work, where the star motifs have been turned under and slip stitched/appliqué stitched into place, with added stem stitch.

The appliqué stitch is worked in the same colour as the applied organdie.

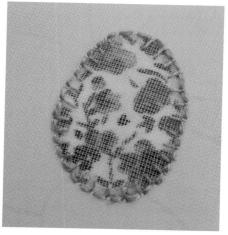

Pin stitch has a straight stitch on the front, worked as a double stitch on the side of the fabric before a vertical stitch is worked creating a slanted stitch on the reverse, which holds the applied fabric in place.

worked in either direction: right-handed stitchers usually work from left to right; left-handers from right to left. The back-stitches need to be equal in size and length to ensure an even herringbone is achieved.

The back of the work shows the neatness of stitch and the edges of the fabric pushed underneath.

REVERSE OR CUTWORK APPLIQUÉ

Reverse appliqué is made of layers of fabric stitched together and then cut to reveal an underneath layer. This method, also known as Mola appliqué, was developed by the Curia Indians, off the coast of Panama. They used designs inspired by their body art, animals and plants. Mythological motifs and ornamental designs were used in bright, contrasting colours of fine cotton fabrics.

More recent examples of reverse/cutwork appliqué are often abstract in design: stripes or squares, perhaps, with more motifs or embroidery added on top of the layers, or the layers can be stitched over with a motif pattern, perhaps a repeating shell or wineglass pattern, or a row of paisley; then each part of this motif is cut away to reveal different layers of fabric. Usually the same motif would have the same fabric cut away to give a consistent pattern.

The pattern can be drawn onto the top layer of fabric using an air-soluble pencil or water-soluble pen. Be careful in your choice of fabric for the top layer, as a smooth, flat surface will make it much easier to trace through the design or to draw around the pattern piece. If a design is particularly detailed, tracing over the design will be easiest, so a light fabric is best.

Choice of fabrics

Remember when layering fabrics it can be best to use lighter weight fabrics, such as silks and cottons, as they will stay flat and allow for more layers where required.

Shell pattern is often used in English quilting, and can be very effective as a pattern for cutwork.

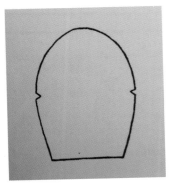

Template shape for shell pattern.

Wineglass pattern, also used in English quilting originally, but most effective within appliqué too.

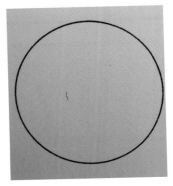

Template shape for wineglass pattern.

Clutch bag using cutwork appliqué as the base fabric, covered with machine-stitched canvas.

The canvas weft threads have been removed and the warp threads covered in machine zigzag

The handle of the bag is worked in layers of fabric, machine stitched and cut to reveal underneath layers.

Edges on cutwork appliqué can be left raw, against the stitching, or they can be turned under (as seen in many quilts). The fabric layers can be attached using machine running stitch, or a zigzag stitch can be used to hide the raw edges more efficiently. Alternatively a hand stitch – backstitch or similar – can be used, or a satin stitch to give a denser, more substantial edge line. It is probably more usual to see this technique worked with machine rather than hand stitching as it is really the cutwork that is the main event, not the running stitch. A machine allows for a greater area of fabric to be covered quickly and the fabrics also tend to behave well under the machine foot, being trapped down quickly and efficiently.

The Mola technique also uses two or more layers of colour-contrasting fabrics, laid on top of each other and sewn together at the edges. Beginning with the top layer of fabric, the shape of the motif is now cut out and the edges of each shape sewn by hand to the layer beneath. Each cut reveals the colour of the next layer of fabric. Larger motifs are cut in the top layer rather than in the underlying layers so that a brightly coloured, stepped effect is produced. The motif is worked in this way from the top downwards – this is therefore known as 'reverse appliqué'. Smaller pieces of fabric are also added between the layers for extra colour and lines too fine to be added with fabric pieces are embroidered on top using matching threads, much like the more modern pieces of reverse/cutwork appliqué. Some of the most effective fabrics for this technique are thin silk and dupion as these can fray nicely and be layered to good effect, but of course cottons and organzas can also give good colours and layering as well. Thicker, more textured fabrics can be used, although these might not allow for so many layers; felts give a smoother, neater but less textured effect. Try contrasting fabrics where design motifs are very different but perhaps keep fabrics more similar if a background is being worked rather than a design so that it doesn't 'fight' against the image on top.

Detail of stitched canvas.

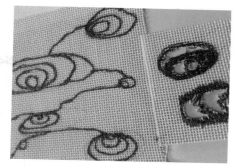
Straight stitches worked over canvas, before being cut into.

Cutwork is all worked in layers of silk dupion with a padded felt motif on top. The contrast of fabrics used helps to bring the rose motif to the foreground and the matt felts against the shiny silks also help identify the two areas.

BRODERIE PERSE

Broderie perse is the French name given to Persian embroidery, a style of appliqué embroidery that uses printed elements and motifs to create a new scene or composition onto a usually plain background fabric. It was most popular in Europe in the seventeenth century, probably having travelled from India and gained popularity in England during the eighteenth century, as it offered an economical way of re-using often expensively imported chintz.

Broderie perse does not use any padding, so motif shapes are cut out and applied straight to the background. Motifs can overlap or sit next to one another with space in between, depending on the design.

Broderie perse tends to either turn under the edges of each motif being applied, and then a slip/appliqué stitch is used to attach the motif to the background fabric, or to use a buttonhole and satin stitch without turning under the edges first. A design would probably use either one or other of these stitch techniques, rather than combing the stitched edge with a turned-under edge.

The turned-under edge is worked much like in quilting techniques where a motif is applied, leaving about 5mm–1cm around the printed motif (depending on its size) before cutting it out and using machine thread to make small stitches, pushing under the excess fabric as one moves around the motif. The edges can all be pinned under before commencing the stitching, but this is a less usual practice. Use lace pins or ento pins so that the fabric does not mark and just make sure that the turned-under edge does not show through the fabric.

A typical scene of boats in a style that was often adapted to broderie perse.

Motifs pinned in position before stab stitching in place.

Stab stitches are worked in machine thread and a small embroidery needle, usually either a No. 12 or 10 but can be bigger if you are finding it hard to thread through the small eye.

This design uses both buttonhole and satin stitch, shading the thread to match the motifs. Satin stitch is used to give the vase a denser appearance while the buttonhole stitch is quite close to cover the frayed edges.

Broderie perse was also known as 'chintz appliqué', where printed flowers and other flora and fauna motifs were applied onto a solid fabric background. Buttonhole and satin stitch was often used within chintz appliqué, matching the thread colour to the colour on the motif at the edge being worked.

Before the buttonhole or satin stitch is worked, small stab stitches in machine thread are worked, as usual, coming up in the background fabric and down over the edge of the motif fabric being applied. The size and length of stitch is as always a few millimetres, but again this depends on the size of the motif. The printed motif should have about 2–3mm excess fabric around it before the cut line as this will allow for the stab stitches to sit on the fabric but not interfere with the motif. If the fabric motifs are prone to fraying (for example if a duck cotton or heavier fabric is being used) then longer, bigger stab stitches may be necessary.

A variety of fabrics and threads can be used for broderie perse: cottons are a good weight of fabric and don't fray if being turned under. Other more frayable fabrics are fine too but better in this case to use buttonhole and satin stitch edge rather than trying to turn them under, especially as the turn under wants to be about 5mm–1cm (no more or it begins to look bulky, especially if the motif is small). Stranded cottons always work really well for satin stitch but more twisted threads, like perlé, can be very effective when used in buttonhole. If the stitch requires a smooth, even effect (like a satin stitch or closed buttonhole), stranded cotton or *ver à soie* is a good choice. If, however, the stitch lines need to be defined and make up a pattern (such as a feather stitch or an open buttonhole) then a perlé or similar slightly thicker twisted thread can look more effective.

Buttonhole stitch used on broderie perse.

Satin stitch used on broderie perse.

Stitch direction should follow the shape that is being worked.

INLAY APPLIQUÉ

Inlay appliqué was popular in the nineteenth century, used to make banners and altar cloths from inlaid brocade and velvet, couched in gold cord. It was sometimes known as 'mosaic work' and has been described as being a link between patchwork and appliqué. It also has similarities to reverse appliqué, although there are several different methods that can be used. Machine inlay or decoupé method uses two pieces of fabric stitched together around the outline of a design. The design is then cut away from the top fabric to reveal the motif on the fabric below, very like reverse appliqué does. Meanwhile applied inlay adds panels of contrasting fabric to the basic or reverse appliqué, with the idea of creating the illusion of inlaid work. Seen from a distance it is very effective.

Inlay appliqué is the opposite of onlay appliqué. Onlay appliqué (as explored in the previous chapters) is the technique of applying one fabric to another and edging to these motifs as required. Inlay appliqué applies areas of fabric next to each other rather than on top of one another and tends to use felt on top of a linen or cotton backing. The backing is often not seen but purely used as a base on which to lay the pieces of felt, much like a jigsaw puzzle.

The preparation for this technique is the most important part. The design is traced onto tracing paper and each piece is cut out and transferred onto the felt. The felt pieces need to be cut out with care and precision so that they fit together once transferred to the backing fabric. The felt can sometimes shrink, so may need to be cut slightly bigger than the pattern pieces and then trimmed if necessary once in place. Anything with too much detail, or too many edges, will

Successful motif shapes

Broderie perse is most effective when simple shaped motifs are used. Smooth, round edges are much easier to cover or turn under than jagged, sharp lines and lots of turns. Avoid holly leaves and embrace roses!

An example of felt inlay appliqué, using leaf motifs to create a pattern that fits together.

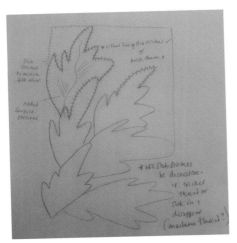

Working sketch for the inlay appliqué design.

A coloured sketch to work out which shades work next to one another.

A design taken from a design based on waves and used as a cutwork appliqué. It would also work really well as inlay, because of its simple lines and block colours.

Stab stitches are usually worked in whatever thickness of thread is desired, coming out of the background and onto the felt motif.

A variety of surface stitches can be added on top to embellish the design, including fly and feather stitch, and couched thread.

handmade varieties but the main thing is that all the felt used in the design is of the same weight. The idea of felt inlay, as the word suggests, is that the felt is flat like wood inlay on furniture or a mosaic made from tiles. The finished result should be flat and smooth, with all fabrics lying next to one another at one level.

QUILTING APPLIQUÉ

This book does not look at all the quilting methods of appliqué, which is really a whole subject in itself. One technique used by quilt makers which might be useful to consider within embroidered appliqué, however, is the freezer paper method of applying motifs. This method helps to keep the turned-under edges around the whole motif fixed before it is applied to the background fabric. Sometimes spray starch or basting is also used. It usually gives a very smooth edge, which can then be applied with slip stitches/appliqué stitches to the foundation or backing fabric.

be harder to fit together; however, there are no turned-under or frayed edges to worry about, so the design can be as simple or complicated as desired. There is a wonderful example in Gail Marsh's book, *Early 20th Century Embroidery Techniques*, of two inlay felt tigers amongst the jungle leaves on a linen background, worked in the 1920s by Alice Edna Smith. It shows

how bright, bold colours worked within a clear picture or design work brilliantly for this technique. It is particularly good for showing clear demarcation between each felt piece, to give an almost cartoon-like, pop-art image.

It can be a good idea to draw the design first, and perhaps paint or colour in different areas to work out the light and dark tones and placements. It can help to do the design in paper first, not only to check the colours work next to each other but also the shape of all the pieces, so that they work and fit together easily once cut out and put together in felt. Thin craft felt is a bit easier to use than the thicker or

This bird motif has been worked by Mags McCosher using the freezer paper method.

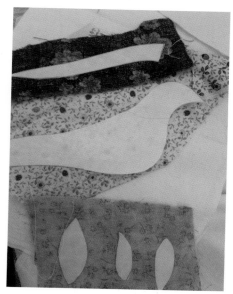

The motifs are cut out of freezer paper and pinned to the fabric. Keep in mind grain and pattern of the fabric and how you want that to appear within each shape or motif. Cotton fabric is best, as anything too thick will be bulky. The idea is to keep fabrics all the same so that once applied you cannot tell if the fabric is one or several.

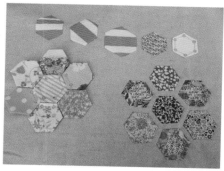

Simple traditional covered hexagons are applied to the background linen making up a more abstract design.

This method is best used for simple shapes, nothing too small or complicated. It is particularly useful when bulk of fabrics is not required. The applied shapes have the background fabric removed from underneath them so that the work is as flat as possible, giving a similar effect as if it were one continuous piece of fabric.

In Mags McCosher's samples, the large stitches are tacking lines, to hold the layers of fabric and wadding in place, under which equally sized running stitch has been worked using the 'rocking' method rather than taking the needle in and out as we do for embroidery. The shapes are simple but effective, especially by the colours and patterns that have been used and put together. The overall effect is smooth and seamless, allowing any running stitch that is quilted on top (as shown on the three-dimensional brick pattern) to be smooth and flat.

It is important that the glue is not permanent, as the freezer paper needs to be taken out from the back of the motifs once they are stitched down to the backing fabric. The glue is a much quicker way to attach the fabric around the paper, rather than stitching side to side, as you would do when paper piecing in patchwork quilts, covering hexagons with fabric by taking small catching stitches around each corner. It also allows the fabric to be pulled little by little and the idea is that it gives a smoother turn, which can then be stitched down.

The fabric is cut leaving a margin around the freezer paper of about 5mm, but this slightly depends on the size of the motif. Use a water-soluble glue stick to attach the excess fabric to the freezer paper.

Attach the motifs using slip stitch/appliqué stitch with a fine machine cotton. Most quilters prefer cotton to polyester because it matches the fabric being used. The colour of the thread should match that of the fabrics being used, so that stitches become as invisible as possible.

The flower has been worked in the same way as the bird motif: each petal has been applied separately and then stem stitch and lazy daisies have been worked on top, using stranded cottons.

These samples, by Mags McCosher, have been worked in the same way, showing parts that make up a larger quilt.

Once all parts of the design have been stitched to the background fabric the piece can be turned to the reverse and the background fabric can be cut away, leaving a 5mm or so margin around each motif. The freezer paper can be removed by simply wetting the area, which will remove the water soluble glue, allowing the paper to come away easily.

STAINED GLASS APPLIQUÉ

The name of this type of appliqué has more to do with its appearance than a particular technique. Like a stained glass window, it is made up of bright, coloured pieces of fabric surrounded by black strips of fabric, usually bias binding, or lines of satin stitch. Two methods are used: the crossway and the overlay. The crossway method uses bias strips, i.e. strips of fabric cut on the bias (the diagonal of the fabric), which allows for stretch and manipulation around shapes more easily and smoothly than if the fabric were to be cut straight against the grain. It is important that the strips are all equal in width throughout the design, to give an even impression.

Motifs that are too small or intricate still do not work well within this method, however. The overlay method is another form of reverse/cutwork appliqué where a dark fabric is put on top of coloured fabric and then cut away to reveal the coloured fabric beneath.

Drawing of a design for stained glass appliqué. The coloured sections are to be attached to the background fabric using Bondaweb and then using the crossway method, bias binding is to be slip stitched along each design line, between the coloured blocks.

This fabric sample gives a similar impression as that of stained glass. It shows how fabrics can be used as a starting point for design, or as a basis on which to put one's appliqué and embroidery.

Detail of Mags McCosher's quilt, showing how the stained glass effect can be used with patterned fabrics.

A running stitch has been worked around the edges of the borders, which helps to push them forward and make them even more prominent.

An antique example of Carrickmacross lace from Jenny Adin-Christie's collection.

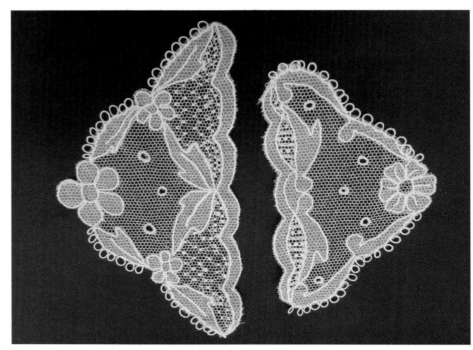

A beautiful example of modern Carrickmacross by Jenny Adin-Christie.

APPLIQUÉ ON NET

Appliqué on net is also known as Carrickmacross lace, as was used on the Duchess of Cambridge's wedding dress to great effect. It originated in the early 1820s, in Carrickmacross and other Irish towns, and was first known as cambric appliqué or Limerick cut cambric until the 1870s when it became widely referred to as Carrickmacross. It was inspired by the Italian lace of that time, tending to be made by the poor for the rich, and was an important part of the rural income. The lace was worked by applying fine organdie to a delicate net ground. Once complete the excess organdie is cut away to reveal the design. A further effect called 'guipure' links areas of the pattern, without the use of net, to create an intricate design of open work, using all sorts of stitches such as bars and cobwebs that fill and add interest. The designs were often of simple flowers and foliage. It is often used on veils and garments, and particularly for wedding and christening attire, partly perhaps because it is usually white on white and very delicate.

FURTHER APPLIQUÉ TECHNIQUES

Lace stitch appliqué
This uses a three-sided stitch (or lace stitch) to attach the motif at the edges. It is often used on lingerie.

Freehand machine appliqué
The teeth are lowered on the sewing machine to allow the stitcher to move up and down, left and right as required to give more sketchy stitching around an applied motif. Poppy Treffry is a good example of an artist who uses this technique to great effect.

Here trailing has been used in a similar way to a lace stitch, cutting away fabric against the stitch to leave paper and tissue organdie in this case, much like the method used with lace and silk on lingerie.

Three-dimensional detached shapes can add height without the need for padding underneath.

zigzag machine edges worked over a tissue paper star for a Christmas card design, stitched in metallic machine thread.

Simple motifs have been applied using machine running stitch, leaving some frayed edges showing and some completely stitched over.

Design for how these shapes could be used.

Machine-stitched appliqué

Appliqué that is sewn solely by machine has different qualities from hand-worked appliqué. It is bold and basic and usually quicker therefore to execute. It produces strong seams and can be useful for heavier fabrics and where articles or pieces of work are used for garments, bags or other items that might need washing frequently. The main stitch used for machine appliqué is probably the zigzag stitch, set close to form a solid line and to resemble a satin stitch. This stitch attaches an applied motif securely and covers any frayed edges completely.

Machine stitches can also be used to make detached shapes, much like those we use in raised and stumpwork. These can be simple wire laid on top of a shape and then a zigzag stitch on top to cover the wire and the raw edge of the fabric.

Once stitched the excess fabric around the edge of the machine stitching can be cut away to leave the shape. Wadding can be sandwiched between two layers of fabric to create a more padded motif or organza can be used to create a lighter, more translucent three-dimensional motif.

Mixed media appliqué

A combination of materials and techniques is used in mixed media appliqué, including fraying, spray-starching, batik, burning, machine embroidery, dyeing and hand painting using a mixture of wood, metal, wire, paper, mirrors, sequins, feathers and beads. Printed fabrics can be combined with an odd button as the head of a flower, or a sequin on a Christmas tree. Paint and paper can be used in conjunction with stitch to create endless possibilities.

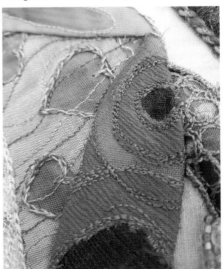

Shadow underlay is combined with rose petals and machine embroidery before being cut out and attached over padding.

Bondaweb is helpful for more complicated shapes.

Jennifer Donovan's piece shows how pleated and gathered fabric can be stitched over and around to create raised areas without the need for any padding underneath.

Suffolk puffs show gathered fabric in rounds and circles, without the need for any padding.

Fused or bonded appliqué

This technique is used as an alternative to stitching, usually for small motifs, perhaps complicated in shape and used on pieces of work that are not being used and handled often if at all. More often though, this method is used as a preparation to stitching rather than as an independent method. Bonding has been used as a preparation for appliqué embroidery for centuries. The modern equivalents of the early starches and pastes are much easier to use and come in many different forms (as previously mentioned in the Materials chapter) and include fusible fabric adhesives, such as Bondaweb, to iron on interfacing material, which is sandwiched between the layers of fabric. Fusible interfacings have a variety of uses: knitted and loosely woven fabrics, such as hessian, can be made easier to work with by lining them with a fusible material in order to stiffen the fabric and prevent stretching. Also, by fusing light-coloured interfacing to the back of a light-coloured fabric, it can then be applied to a dark background without the background colour showing through. Interfacing comes in different weights, so it can also be used to thicken thin or lightweight fabrics. It has lots of helpful uses, but it is best to use it sparingly if possible because it is ultimately a glue, so it does change the movement of a fabric; although helpful it can sometimes take away from the effect too.

Making a Suffolk puff

Cut a circle, using a template or a mug or plate to draw around. The circle needs to be about twice as big as the finished puff size required.

Turn a small edge onto the wrong side of the fabric and catch this edge down using machine cotton and a fine embroidery needle, making a running stitch all the way around the circle.

Pull the running stitch tightly to pull the gathers together and finish the thread underneath. Or the same thread can be used to attach the puff to the background fabric.

Suffolk puffs can be made in various sizes, but work best using a fine fabric, such as a cotton lawn, which will pleat nicely and easily.

Manipulated fabrics

Some exciting effects can be achieved by manipulating, pleating and folding fabrics, creating new textures and shapes for backgrounds and applied areas.

It can be a good idea to try small samples first, using different fabrics depending on the effect that is desired. Chiffons and cotton lawn fabrics will pleat, ruche and drape easily while linens and cottons will fold better into sharp pleats and tucks, creating more linear and definite lines. Frayed edges can be useful to create tufts and areas of embroidery stitches can flatten out the gathers. A smocking machine can be another useful tool to use where even gathers are required or a running stitch by machine or hand can create even or uneven results. If the row of stitches follows a zigzag rather than straight pattern, a scalloped edging effect is achieved. If formed in a circle, gathers are created in a round, rather like a Suffolk puff.

Suffolk puffs

The Suffolk puff is a simple circle of fabric that is gathered together by small running stitches. As the name suggests it comes from the county of Suffolk, although in America it is known as a 'yo-yo'! Suffolk puffs have been around since the 1600s but were particularly popular on quilts in the Victorian era, using scraps of fabric to make the puffs before being sewn together. The technique may have been named after the fact that the puffs were often stuffed with Suffolk sheep wool, although usually these days they are not stuffed, but the gathers give them that appearance of puff and height.

These Suffolk puffs can be a great addition to appliqué textile pieces, also onto a garment or onto a quilt. But they can also be stitched together to form necklaces and collars or other decoration on garments, by sewing the edges together where they meet.

Fabrics can be moulded by treating with a watered down PVA glue or starch. Wallpaper paste and plaster of Paris can also be used, but it is worth bearing in mind if any stitching needs to be added to these fabrics, to ensure that the needle will go through the moulded fabrics without too much trouble. (Pliers may be helpful for this!) Hessians and canvas fabrics, linens and scrim all work well and can be used over moulds, such as jars and bowls, to create shapes that hold once dry.

Edges of man-made fabric can also be sealed before being stitched down and used in much the same way as frayed edges. Synthetic fabrics work well if swiftly held over a flame, as they act much like plastic to create a solid, black seal. Natural fibres tend not to seal in the same way, but do not burn as quickly.

⁂ CHAPTER 8 ⁂

FINISHING OFF

She watched and taught the girls that sang at their embroidery frames
while the great silk flowers grew from their needles.

– LOUISE JORDAN MILN: THE FEAST OF LANTERNS (1920)

Once your appliqué embroidery is complete it can be a difficult decision to know what to do with it. A picture perhaps, a brooch, a cushion, bunting, a bookmark, a notebook or a needlecase – these are just a few ideas. This chapter explores how to mount a piece of finished embroidery and also how to make up your embroidery into simple finished pieces to use or to decorate. Appliqué can be used in lots of other ways too: on garments, as a box lid, on the front cover of a book, as a decoration, as a soft wall hanging – the list goes on. But whatever you choose to do with the finished piece of work, it is really important that the finishing off or making up complements the work and doesn't detract from it. When such a long time is spent on the design, the appliqué and the embroidery, it is important to finish it well!

MOUNTING

- -

Most embroidery pieces of work are mounted and some picture framers will do this for you. There are two main ways of mounting pieces of work that are best for embroidery, both of which avoid the use of glue directly on the work itself. The herringbone method is the most thorough but lacing is a good, quicker alternative method to use. Another difference is that herringbone is stitched along the edge of the board on each side while lacing goes across the whole board, one way or both ways as needed. The most important thing to remember is that the embroidery needs to be mounted tight over the board so that the background fabric is taut, smooth and wrinkle free.

If the embroidery consists of mostly applied lightweight fabrics with little or no plunging of threads to the back, then the work does not need to sit on a layer of wadding or domette (something soft that the threads will sink into to prevent bumps on the front). If, however, lots of

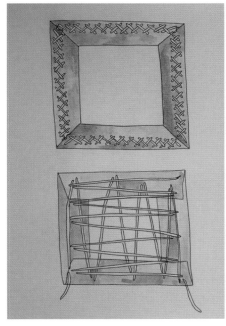

Herringbone and lacing techniques are both suitable for most embroidery.

metal threads have been used for couching, requiring plunging of threads to the back, a layer of something soft will be needed between the card and the piece of embroidery.

OPPOSITE: Prayer flags hanging up.

Gimp is taken over the edges of the board at the corners and lies behind the sateen rather than being plunged as normal. This keeps the sides neat and smooth.

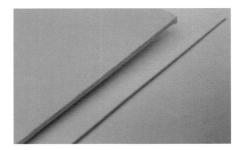

Grade A mountboard is thicker than Grade C.

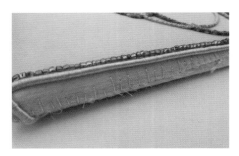

The edges of the applied fabrics are hidden from sight around the back of the mountboard.

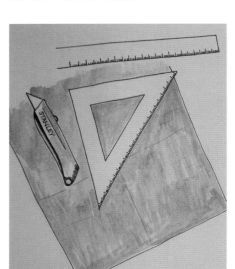

Equipment for cutting mountboard.

Usually the embroidery is pulled over a piece of mountboard. It comes in different thicknesses and the most common is Grade C: this really needs two layers to ensure that it doesn't bend when the embroidery is pulled over it. Grade A is a thicker mountboard and therefore only one layer is needed, but it is more expensive. Choose acid-free mountboard, as this protects the work. A layer of calico (or cotton fabric) is usually stretched over the board first to act as a barrier between the card and embroidery, but it is also an essential part of mounting when using the herringbone method.

Hardboard and foam-core board are also sometimes used for mounting. Hardboard is a good alternative if the work is heavy and needs something substantial to wrap around, while foam-core board is much lighter weight, so can be useful for pieces that use very lightweight fabric and threads, such as shadow-work or whitework. Acid-free mountboard usually comes in white, as does foam-core board; hardboard is usually brown.

To find the size of board required there are many decisions to be made. Usually a piece of embroidery will want a margin of about 4–5cm around the four outside edges to give it some space and 'room to breathe'. However, this measurement will vary depending on the size of the embroidery and in some cases the design may need more space or background fabric at the bottom or around a corner of the design. Sometimes it may not require any space around it, so that it is mounted up to the work; this is particularly suitable for appliqué work, as any raw edges of applied fabric can be hidden away by stretching them around the board.

It is important to remember that if you are using two pieces of Grade C mountboard, they need to be cut to exactly the same size! It is best to use a cutting mat and a sharp Stanley or craft knife for this job and a strong metal ruler and set square

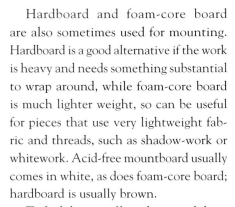

Cutting mountboard

Keep the ruler on the inside of the board so that if the knife veers off it does not cut the board being used. Do not press down too hard with the knife; several cuts along the same line will give a better result than one or two heavy cuts, as you have more control over the knife when it is not too firmly pushed down into the card.

to ensure measurements are correct and that the knife doesn't veer off in a different direction!

The mountboard is first covered in calico, using glue – either conservation glue, which is odourless, a little like PVA, and takes a few seconds to hold so pins are usually needed to hold the fabric while it dries, or Copydex, which has a very strong smell and does turn yellow with age. It is more gum-like and stretchy in texture but holds immediately. Both are fine, as the glue is applied at the back of the board, not the front where the embroidery sits, but conservation glue is probably a less aggressive adhesive to use. Stretch the calico as tightly as possible over the card. The piece of embroidery will only be as tight as the calico; slack or baggy calico will result in a baggy piece of embroidery once mounted!

Gluing calico onto mountboard

Glue is put on the two opposite edges, about 2cm away from the edge, depending on the size of the board.

The drawing shows how the corners are cut to take out any bulk from the calico.

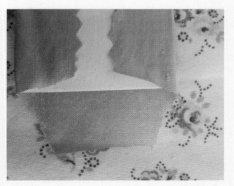

Once the corners are cut, glue is put onto the two remaining opposite sides.

If a piece of work does need a piece of wadding or domette between the piece of work and the board, to allow any plunged threads to sink into, then this can be put on top of the calico now, before the embroidery is pinned on top. Simply lay the wadding on top of the covered calico board and, using fabric scissors, cut through the wadding at a slight angle, against the edge of the board so that the wadding is cut to the same size as the board but possibly a millimetre or two bigger. Slant away from the board when cutting to avoid a ridge of wadding showing underneath the fabric. It is not necessary to put the wadding underneath the calico as this stretches it and makes it firmer. The idea of the wadding is to allow a soft base for the threads to sink into. It also shouldn't need gluing to the calico as it does slightly catch onto it and will then of course be held in place by the piece of embroidery. Different thicknesses of wadding and domette are available, so you can choose what height

is appropriate depending on the thickness of threads plunged and the effect that is desired: more puffy or flatter.

Once the calico has been glued to the board (the same method applies, whichever type of board you use), the next step is to take the embroidery off the frame and pin it onto the board.

Before taking the embroidery off your frame, it can be a good idea to measure it, as this is easier to do when it is stretched. Sometimes this isn't possible to do if the piece has been worked in a ring frame or with background fabric rolled up, but where possible it is helpful to do this now.

Often picture framers will give a piece of work slightly more space at the bottom than at the top and sides. This is because of the optical illusion that occurs when a piece of work is on the wall. For example, if a piece has 5cm around the top and sides, it might be given 7cm along the bottom, which when hanging up will look equal around all four sides. It isn't really

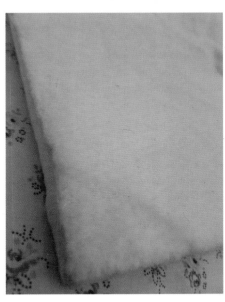

Wadding (in this case domette) sits securely on top of the calico and underneath the embroidery to absorb any plunged threads or lumps and bumps underneath the embroidery.

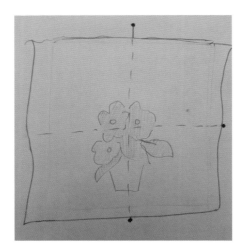

Plume lines can be a good way of making sure the work is placed centrally onto the board.

Pin along opposite sides, allowing enough space that the embroidery can be moved or shifted if need be, to make it more even around any of the sides.

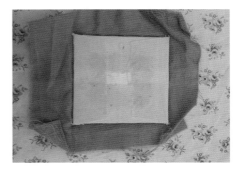

The reverse of the work. Enough fabric should be left around the outside to turn and stitch the herringbone through.

The corners need to be mitred so that they remain as flat and neat as possible underneath the sateen.

necessary to do this at the mounting stage, but at the framing stage it can be a good idea, especially where a cut mount is used.

Once the embroidery is measured, another good thing to do before taking it off the frame, is either to put two plume lines along the piece to find the central point or, perhaps easier and as efficient, decide on the halfway points for each side. Simply measure each side and pop a pin halfway along each side and at the top and bottom. Once the calico is glued to the board, the sides and top and bottom can also be measured and a small pencil mark put on the side edge of each four sides. Simply match up the pins with the pencil marks to ensure that the piece of work has been put onto the board centrally.

These marks and pins should tally up to allow the work to sit flat and central before beginning to pin around the edge of the board. Glass-headed pins are best for this job, as they are not too flimsy but have a firm head and a suitable length and thickness to them. Firstly pin the opposite sides, leaving a good 4cm between pins. Once opposite sides are pinned, top and bottom can be done in the same way. Pull tight but not really tight at this stage.

Once you are happy with the placement of the embroidery and the spaces look even between the embroidery and the background fabric on all sides, then more pins can be added. It is always best to work opposite sides as this encourages the fabric to be taut and not to 'walk'. If the space between the embroidery and edge of the card is uneven on one side, fabric can be shifted one pin at a time in the direction required.

Once all the pins are in, placed about 1cm apart, and the fabric is pulled as tightly as possible to remove any puckers or bumps in the fabric, you are then almost ready to start the herringbone or the lacing on the back. First it is a good idea to fold and pin all four corners so that they are mitred and ready to be stitched, particularly with a small piece of work, in order to avoid any difficulty – although this isn't a hard and fast rule. Some prefer to fold each corner as they come to it while herringboning, but this can mean that it is difficult to push the fabric underneath the corner if the herringbone stitches have gone too close to a corner.

Mitred corners

- It can be helpful to pin the fabric so that the right angle is kept while folding and manipulating the corner into a mitre.
- Start with one side, making sure the fold of the fabric runs along the edge of the board, not slanting away or up from the edge.
- Make sure the fold of the mitre sits exactly in the middle of the corner, not sliding off it.
- Repeat with the other side and pin both in place top and bottom to ensure no movement while herringboning.
- The mitre on either side should sit next to each other without a big open gap. Try not to overlap the corner (it doesn't matter if the fabric overlaps further up from the corner as this can be cut away afterwards).

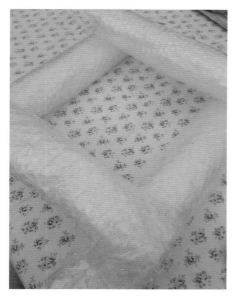

The bubble wrap frame sits just inside the board, allowing the edge of the embroidery to sit just on it, all the way round.

When lacing work opposite side to opposite side, keep an even gap. The size of the gap depends on the piece of work, but around 1–2cm is usual. The lacing has been worked both ways to ensure the embroidery remains taut.

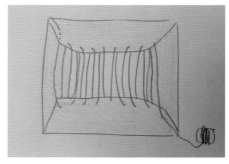

Small stitches are worked to finish the thread and the thread can go through its own loop to make a knot if desired.

Once all the pins are attached into the board and corners are mitred the embroidery needs to be turned front down. If it is fairly flat, it can simply be rested onto a piece of acid-free tissue or an old clean sheet or pillowcase or piece of fabric – this keeps it clean and protected from the table and gives a little bit of softness. However, if the piece of work has padded areas and areas with fragile thread, such as metal purls or wired shapes, or just high areas of carpet and felt padding, then these will not want to sit directly on the table. The best thing to do is to make four rolls out of bubble wrap (wadding or domette can work too) and make a frame on which the work can sit. This protects the embroidery from being squashed or flattened while the herringbone or lacing is worked.

LACING METHOD

This is a quicker, less efficient but perfectly acceptable way to mount the work. Using buttonhole thread, but keeping it on the spool rather than cutting a length, it needs to be threaded through a curved or straight embroidery needle. A curved needle is useful for the herringbone method as it helps lift up through the calico, and stops the needle catching on the card, but when lacing the needle is only going through the piece of work, not the calico underneath. Sometimes when lacing, calico is not glued onto the card either, although it is probably advisable to mount over calico or cotton as it does protect the embroidery.

Lacing a piece of work is a bit like playing a harp, as once a few lines have been put in, the thread needs pulling to allow more thread free in the needle! Once one side is completed, finish off with a few overstitches through the calico and then tighten, tighten, tighten in the same way

as before, and finish the thread off with a few overstitches at the other end. The card should not bow too much, but these lacing stitches do need to be tight, with no give in them, to ensure a tightly stretched piece of embroidery. Repeat on opposite sides of the work, crossing over the previous lacing.

Lacing can also be worked over herringbone where the embroidery may still be slack, despite being herringboned taut. Usually this would not need lacing throughout the back of the board but just in one place to tighten a bump or part of baggy fabric within the design.

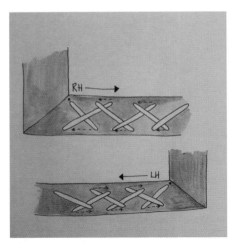

Drawing of herringbone stitch, worked by a right-handed stitcher (RH) and a left-handed stitcher (LH), worked in opposite directions.

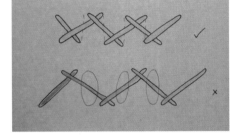

It doesn't matter very much about the size of herringbone stitches but they do need to sit parallel, so that all the fabric is covered. If the stitches are too far apart they leave areas of fabric unstitched.

Keeping herringbone stitches tight

It can be easier to stitch first and then worry about tightening the stitches with a mellor when the thread needs finishing, rather than trying to get them really tight as you go, stitch by stitch.

Slip stitching along the corner means the stitches will not show if the sateen is put on slightly high, away from the corner. It also ensures the work is attached firmly around all four corners.

HERRINGBONE METHOD

It is important to use buttonhole thread both for lacing and herringboning, as it is a strong thread and doesn't break easily under the pressure of being pulled tight. It doesn't need to be doubled up: single thread is fine – although some prefer it double. Usually a cream colour is used as this matches the card and calico colour, so it sinks in easily without showing. If a dark colour sateen is used behind the piece then a dark buttonhole could be used, just so long as the stitches are not going to show through the sateen or alternative backing, which may look untidy.

Use a big enough needle to thread the buttonhole without difficulty; the very fine curved needles are great for slip stitching the sateen onto the back of the board once the herringbone is completed but can break if used for stitching the herringbone, due to the pressure that is put on the needle as it hits the card.

Start with a knot and a few overstitches through the calico, just below the glue line, probably 2cm away from the edge of the card and 6cm or so away from a corner. Herringbone stitches can be worked evenly until the corner is reached. Stitch size does vary depending on the size of the piece of work, but the main thing is to keep herringbone stitches next to each other without a gap between each cross.

When a corner is reached, use a mellor or a blunt big tapestry needle to pull the herringbone stitches tight. It is always surprising how much thread will be gained by doing this. It is also a good idea to do this before finishing off a thread. Herringbone stitch uses a lot of thread so there will be a fair amount of finishing and starting of thread! The calico should look tight and flat underneath the herringbone stitches; if it doesn't, the stitches may not be pulled tight enough.

If the buttonhole thread gets caught repeatedly around the pins, a piece of paper or a length of fabric can be slid under the work or wrapped over the pins, to cover them so that the thread can't catch on them. Buttonhole thread can be cut quite long for herringbone stitch, rather than following the 'wrist to elbow' rule, as the stitch does use a lot of thread up quite quickly. If it is annoying not only because it gets caught around the pins but also because it knots and twists up on itself then do use shorter lengths but you will need to start and finish the thread more often, which is a bit more time consuming.

A slip stitch (sometimes known as a ladder stitch) is used working from the top of the mitre down to the corner.

Once the corner has been slip stitched, continue around the next side until the next corner and repeat until all sides and corners are stitched. At this point the pins can now be taken off. It probably

Castle turrets

It can be helpful to think of the slip stitch like a row of castle turrets, the top turret through one side and the bottom turret through the other side, which are then pulled tightly together. This now looks like one solid line rather than the turret effect.

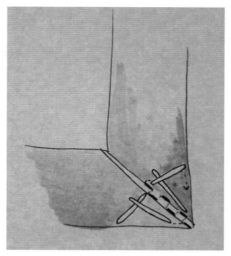

Drawing to illustrate the castle turret effect of slip stitch along a corner.

Cutting away any excess fabric from the back helps the sateen to lie flat.

doesn't make much difference but it can be a good idea, particularly with bigger pieces of work, to take the pins out every other pin at a time, continuously around the board, to allow the fabric to sink in evenly, rather than to take out the pins in sections all together. The pins do not need to be left in until after the sateen is stitched on, as once the herringbone is complete this should be stretched enough to hold the embroidery properly and tightly. The pins also get in the way so it is best to take them out as soon as possible.

It is important to make sure that your needle goes through both the fabric of the embroidery and the calico. The best way to ensure all layers of fabric have been stitched and caught through is to hit the card with your curved needle before coming up to the top of the fabric again.

Keeping the embroidery face down, any excess fabric at the corners can be cut away, to allow the fabric to sit as flat as possible. Also if the embroidery has a large margin over the board after the herringbone stitches then this can also be trimmed down. Be careful not to trim it too close to the herringbone stitches or the fabric will stick up and be less likely to lie as flat underneath the sateen. Best to leave a couple of centimetres after the herringbone stitches; the margin should be fairly equal around all four sides of herringbone.

BACKING FABRIC

Sateen does not really need to be used over the lacing method, as the lacing does not go through any glue, and wraps around the board, but sometimes it is used anyway just to neaten the back of a piece of work. But it is essential when the herringboning method is used. Once the glue disappears (which will take a good number of years!) it is only the sateen that is holding the embroidery tight onto the board, so rather than being necessary for the look and neatness of a piece, it actually becomes really important if a piece has been mounted for a number of years and the glue has disintegrated.

Other fabrics can be used although sateen works particularly well because it has a slight stretch to it. Linens and cottons are also good alternatives and are sometimes chosen to match the fabric on the front, for example a sampler on linen may well use linen on the backing too. It can be argued though that it is not necessary to use an expensive fabric on the back that will not be seen, and something like a silk would

Sateen folds underneath itself and stops along the calico and front fabric edge.

not be as strong or possibly last as long as a cotton or sateen. The sateen comes in various colours but usually the cream is used. It has a slightly shiny surface on the front and a more matt appearance on the back. It also has a diagonal grain on the front which if possible wants to run from bottom left to top right once it is placed on

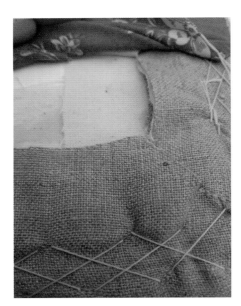

The linen is folded over the board, but with not enough excess to completely cover the calico edge.

1. A slip stitch comes out of the linen and up into the backing fabric, in this case a flower print cotton lawn.

3. Pull slip stitches tight so they disappear.

2. Out of the backing fabric and straight down into the linen.

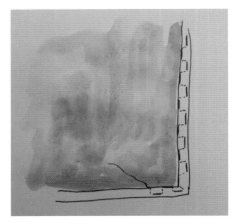

The slip stitches form a 'castle turret' pattern, just the same as when working a corner in the herringbone method of mounting.

the back of the board. This makes it pull better and more evenly. The back of the sateen has a more vertical and horizontal grain to it.

The sateen does not need any mitred corners – phew! It is cut leaving a good 4cm or so around each side from the edge of the board, i.e. the sateen is 4cm bigger around each side than the mountboard. There are different views on the amount of sateen to leave and the measurements here are given as a guide for a standard, medium-sized piece of work. It looks neatest if the sateen excess folds underneath itself and comes to the end of the herringbone stitches, where the calico also ends. If this is repeated on all four sides it gives a very neat finish.

However, if a more expensive fabric such as a linen is being used, you may wish to only leave 3cm around the entire piece as your margin to turn underneath as it still does the desired job, it doesn't look quite so neat as it shows the other layers of fabric underneath but it is functional rather than

for look. The back, after all, is not going to show, but the choice is yours; both ways will effectively hold the embroidery tight.

Fold under opposite sides first and pin at each centre. Make sure the fabric is pulled taut, but better to do too slack and then pull tighter as the sateen marks when folded. It can always be pulled tighter once more pins are added. Then fold in the remaining two sides, pushing in the sides slightly so that they don't show. Pins can be placed just where needed, much further apart than previously used. This keeps the fold smooth.

Use a fine curved needle as the thicker needle will be harder to get through the fold of the fabric. It can be difficult to thread the buttonhole thread but it will go through the needle! Start with a knot above the edge so that it is hidden, and come out of the fold in the sateen a little way from the corner. Stitches are worked much like the slip stitches for the mitred corners. The distance between the stitches is usually about 4mm, but again this does slightly depend on the size of the piece of work. Remember the castle turret pattern for the slip stitches.

Having stitched through the sateen or backing fabric at the corner, come out and down into the linen and continue slip stitches in the same way.

A small running stitch holds the fabric in place, tightly around the circular board.

When you get to a corner, make sure you come out of the backing fabric (e.g. sateen) and down into the fabric on the board. This will help pull the sateen down towards the board.

Make sure stitches are even and pulled really tight so that they disappear. Stitches should sit directly and exactly above and below each other in order that they become invisible. However, sometimes it can be a helpful trick to come up slightly behind a previous stitch rather than in front of it. Coming up in front will make the stitch show. Once a rhythm is found this can be a restful and satisfying last part of the process to do. Use the same colour thread as fabric to help the stitches disappear.

To finish the thread just take two small stab stitches up above the slip stitches underneath the sateen and bring out on through the board fabric, pulling tight to cut, so that the thread bounces back under the sateen again.

The piece of work is now mounted! If there are still any pin marks along the edges of the fabric, just use a mellor or a thick tapestry needle and rub the fabric gently to encourage the threads to mesh back together.

MOUNTING ONTO A CIRCULAR BOARD

When a circle is required rather than a square or rectangular board, the work can be gathered around the board rather than using herringbone. It can still sit on top of a piece of calico which can cover the board in the same way as before but slits may need to be cut into the edge of the calico to ensure it sticks around the circle smoothly.

Rather than pinning the work in place around the board, simply stitch a running stitch a couple of centimetres away from the finished size (as you would when working a slip) and pull tight to gather the fabric around the circular board. Then lace across the back to keep it all taut.

COVERED EMBROIDERY FRAME

Fabric covered embroidery hoops are a great way to mount or frame something quickly and effectively. There are indeed books dedicated to the 'hoop art' and they are a great way to display small embroideries and craftwork.

Felt works well because it doesn't have any frayed edges to worry about. However if fabric is used, simply do a running stitch around the edge and pull to gather the edges underneath the fabric before pinning in place and oversewing or slip stitching down.

CUSHION COVERS

There are many ways to make up cushions, with the use of zips or the simple envelope-type method. Piping or cords around the edge can be very effective and they can be made on the machine or by hand. The simplest method avoids zips and simply stitches two pieces of overlapping fabrics to the work – front sides together, with a machine running stitch or double running hand stitch around all four sides. It can then be turned inside out and stuffed with a cushion pad that should be just slightly

A strip of fabric is simply wrapped around the top ring only and stitched at either end to keep it in place.

A piece of felt or fabric can be stuck or oversewn onto the back to hide any excess fabric.

Simple cushion cover with an envelope back.

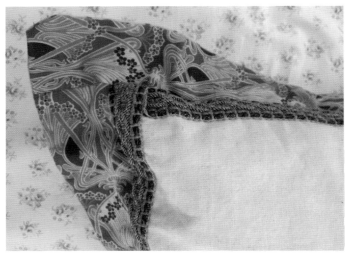

The square can also be stitched much bigger than the cushion pad and then once turned inside out, a running stitch can be worked a few centimetres in to give a flat border.

bigger than the size of the cushion cover, to allow for a good puff.

An edging of buttonhole could be stitched around the edge or a cord, braid, ribbon or piping can be added for extra decoration. Tassels could be made for the corners or lengths of beading. Edges can become as elaborate or simple as you choose.

OTHER IDEAS

A needlecase can be a good way to use a piece of appliqué that is padded, where the padded section can be used for putting pins. It is easily made up much like a booklet, the front in felt so that it needs no edge and isn't too bulky and the inside leaves or pages can be edged in buttonhole, using cotton or a fabric that doesn't give too much bulk so that once closed it is flat and neat. Simple stitches along the fold of the book keep all the pages attached to the cover.

A bookmark is another idea for a small design and can sit over the pages of the book so it doesn't get squashed! A piece of card or Vilene can be inserted between the two layers of fabric to give the bookmark some stiffness.

Appliqué is also a really useful technique to use on garments. Fabrics can be manipulated, folded and pleated before being applied to a jacket collar or a skirt hem. Motifs can also be applied using the transfer method; cutting out the embroidered motif and stab stitching in place before adding a couched line to hide the stab stitches and raw edges. Patches on knees and elbows can be decorative as well as functional by the addition of embroidery and felt is also a good material because it is hard wearing and does not leave a raw edge. Always remember not to apply a heavy fabric to a more lightweight fabric. The background should always be heavier than the fabric being applied to it, so that it all sits comfortably and smoothly.

Think about placement of applied embroidery and motifs, especially on garments. Sometimes it can be worth trying them in different positions first before applying and working out from a practical point of view where they might work best. For example, a beautifully stitched flower motif on an elbow might get worn and damaged quickly, whereas moving it to a shoulder might give it longer lasting durability. Drawings can also be helpful to design and work out placement of applied motifs.

There are also lots of ways of using ready-made items to display one's appliqué embroidery; from box lids to pillowcases and bags – anything can be used. But it may be that the materials used within your appliqué dictate what it is used for: a book cover will need to withstand some handling whereas a framed picture can be as delicate or fragile as the design requires because it does not take any handling. Garments and cushion covers may need to be washed, so this needs to be thought about at the design stage to ensure the appropriate materials are chosen and used.

A needlecase is an easy and effective way to use a simple appliqué design.

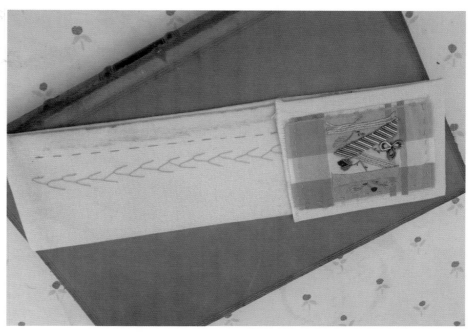

The bookmark is simply made of two pieces of linen stitched right sides together, leaving the bottom open to slide a piece of Vilene or card into before turning in and slip stitching closed. The embroidery is applied onto the top flap at the end, leaving a frayed edge.

Ricrac can make a fun curvy edge: add it in between the two layers of fabric, and stitch the front and back together before turning inside out to show half the ricrac edge.

Boxes can be a really effective way to display your embroidery or appliqué work. The inside of this box is stitched in long and short stitch and three-dimensional flowers are applied to the base of the drawer.

⸭ BIBLIOGRAPHY ⸭

Baker Montano, Judith. *Elegant Stitches*. C&T Publishing, 1995.

Better Homes and Gardens. *Appliqué Class*. John Wiley and Sons, 2011.

Box, Richard. *Colour and Design for Embroidery*. Batsford, 2000.

Brown, Pauline. *Embroidery Skills – Appliqué*. Merehurst 1st, 1989.

Christie, Mrs Archibald. *Samplers and Stitches*. Batsford, 1934.

Clabburn, Pamela. *The Needleworker's Dictionary*. William Morrow, 1976.

De Dillmont, Therese. *Encyclopedia of Needlework*. DMC Library Publications, 1900.

Franklin, Tracy and Nicola Jarvis. *Contemporary Whitework*. Batsford, 2007. (Shadow-work chapter of particular interest.)

Higuchi, Yumiko. *Simply Stitched with Appliqué*. Zakka Workshop, 2017.

Kerrigan, Michael. *Illuminated Manuscripts*. Flame Tree Publishing, 2014.

Mann, Kathleen. *Appliqué: Design and Method*. A&C Black, 1937.

Marsh, Gail. *Early 19th Century Embroidery Techniques*. GMC Publications, 2008.

Marsh, Gail. *Early 20th Century Embroidery Techniques*. GMC Publications, 2011.

Michler, Marsha J. *The Magic of Crazy Quilting*. KP Books, 2003.

Mill, Abigail. *Appliqué Art: Freehand Machine-Embroidered Pictures*. Search Press Ltd, 2014.

Morgan, Margaret. *Bible of Illuminated Letters*. Barron's Educational Series, 2006.

Nakayama-Geraerts, Kumiko. *L'Art du Boutis*. Mango Pratique, 2011.

Pattullo, Mandy. *Textile Collage*. Batsford, 2016.

Stanton, Yvette. *The Left-Handed Embroiderer's Companion*. Vetty Creations, 2010.

Svennas, Elsie. *A Handbook of Lettering for Stitchers*. Van Nostrand-Reinhold, 1973.

Thomas, Mary. *Mary Thomas's Embroidery Book*. Wolfenden Press, 2015.

Thompson, Angela. *Embroiderer's and Quilter's Sourcebook*. Batsford, 2006.

OPPOSITE: Leaf sampler showing inlay appliqué with felt and decorative stitching.

❧ FURTHER READING ❧

Brooks, Susie. *Insect Emporium*. Red Shed, 2016.

Cross, Kate. *Royal School of Needlework: Appliqué: Techniques, Projects and Pure Inspiration*. Search Press, 2016.

Franklin, Tracy A. *New Ideas in Goldwork*. Anova, 2008.

Long, Sophie. *Mastering the Art of Embroidery: Tutorials, Techniques, and Modern Applications*. Chronicle Books, 2013.

Long, Sophie. *Ribbonwork Embroidery: Techniques and Projects*. The Crowood Press, 2017.

Marotta, Millie. *Tropical Wonderland*. Batsford, 2013.

McDonald, Jacqui. *RSN Essential Stitch Guides: Crewelwork*. Search Press, 2010.

Meller, Susan and Joost Elffers. *Textile Designs*. Thames and Hudson, 2002.

Richman, Helen. *Stumpwork Embroidery: Techniques and Projects*. The Crowood Press, 2017.

Sinton, Kate. *RSN Essential Stitch Guides: Stumpwork*. Search Press, 2011.

Wentworth Fitzwilliam, Ada. *Jacobean Embroidery*. General Books LLC, 2010.

Wilson, Erica. *Crewel Embroidery*. Macmillan, 1985.

OPPOSITE: Leaf sampler applied in backstitch.

MATERIALS AND SUPPLIES

Appletons (wools)
www.appletons.org.uk

Benton and Johnson (metal threads)
https://toyekenningandspencer.co.uk/shop/
benton-jonson.html

Crafty Ribbons
www.craftyribbons.com

Golden Hinde (gold threads)
www.golden-hinde.co.uk

John James Needles
www.jjneedles.com

The London Bead Company
www.londonbeadco.com

Sarah Homfray (hand embroidery supplies)
www.sarahhomfray.com

Sew and So
www.sewandso.co.uk

The Silk Route
www.thesilkroute.co.uk

Stef Francis Threads
www.stef-francis.co.uk

Weir Crafts
www.weircrafts.com

Whaleys Bradford Ltd (fabrics)
www.whaleys-bradford.ltd.uk

OPPOSITE: Leaf sampler with couched edges.

[INDEX]

RELATED TITLES FROM CROWOOD

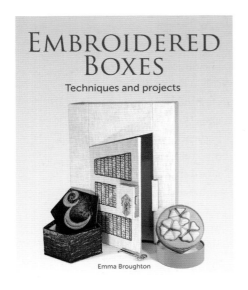

978 1 78500 563 3

978 0 90358 534 7

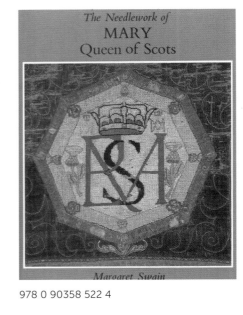

978 0 90358 522 4

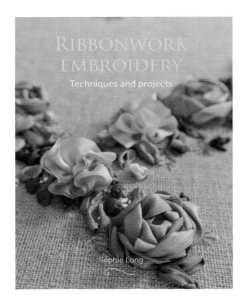

978 1 78500 252 6

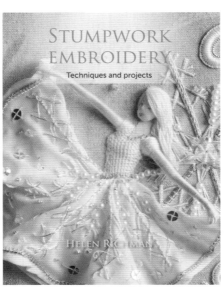

978 1 78500 294 6

978 1 78500 477 3